Center of the Cyclone

by Dr. John C. Lilly

published by Coincidence Control Publishing in Portland, OR

THE CENTER OF THE CYCLONE

The center of the cyclone is that rising quiet central low-pressure place in which one can learn to live eternally. Just outside of this Center is the rotating storm of one's own ego, competing with other egos in a furious high-velocity circular dance. As one leaves center, the roar of the rotating wind deafens one more and more as one joins this dance. One's centered thinking-feeling-being, one's own Satoris, are in the center only, not outside. One's pushed-pulled driven states, one's anti-Satori modes of functioning, one's self-created hells, are outside the center. In the center of the cyclone one is off the wheel of Karma, of life, rising to join the Creators of the Universe, the Creators of us.

Here we find that we have created Them who are Us.

Contents

	Introduction — i
Chapter 1	My first two trips: Exploring LSD spaces and projections — 1
Chapter 2	Near-lethal "accident": "No experiment is a failure" — 22
Chapter 3	Return to the two guides: Tank plus LSD — 37
Chapter 4	Following instructions and going with the flow — 62
Chapter 5	A guided tour of Hell — 92
Chapter 6	Another look at mysticism — 119
Chapter 7	More mysticism: Mentations — 136
Chapter 8	Group workshop at Kairos — 144
Chapter 9	Group rhythm and group resonance at the Kairos workshop — 155
Chapter 10	My first trip to Chile: Oscar Ichazo — 163
Chapter 11	Second trip to Chile: States of consciousness defined — 171
Chapter 12	Physical barriers to positive states: Physical exercises — 186

Chapter 13	State 48: The human biocomputer	193
Chapter 14	State +24: The basic professional state	205
Chapter 15	State +12: The blissful sharing body	210
Chapter 16	State +6: The point as self	237
Chapter 17	State +3: Classical Satori: The Essence as one of the creators	246
Chapter 18	Dyadic Satori: Unity in a couple	256

Epilogue — 261

Acknowledgments — 265

In the Province of My Mind — 267

Toward Equilibration — 270

Recommended Reading — 275

About the Author — 277

Tables

Table 1   Levels of Consciousness and Satori — 175

Table 2   "True" Relationship Between Mentations and Rising Sign — 180

Table 3   Deviated Mentations for Capricorn Rising Sign — 181

Table 4   Deviated Mentations in Terms of Various Rising Signs — 182

Table 5   Schema of the Human Biocomputer — 198

Table 6   Quantitative Relations between Self, Essence and Ego Metaprograms — 202

The Pampas Exercises — 189

Discoveries of any great moment in mathematics and other disciplines, once they are discovered, are seen to be extremely simple and obvious, and make everybody, including their discoverer, appear foolish for not having discovered them before. It is all too often forgotten that the ancient symbol for prenascence of the world is a fool, and that foolishness, being a divine state, is not a condition to be either proud or ashamed of.

Unfortunately, we find systems of education today that have departed so far from the plain truth that they now teach us to be proud of what we know and ashamed of ignorance. This is doubly corrupt. It is corrupt not only because pride is in itself a mortal sin, but also because to teach pride in knowledge is to put an effective barrier against any advance upon what is already known, since it makes one ashamed to look beyond the bonds imposed by one's ignorance.

To any person prepared to enter with respect into the realm of his great and universal ignorance, the secrets of being will eventually unfold, and they will do so in a measure according to his freedom from natural and indoctrinated shame in his respect of their revelation.

In the face of the strong, and indeed violent, social pressures against it, few people have been prepared to take this simple and satisfying course toward sanity. And in a society where a prominent psychiatrist can advertise that, given the chance, he would have treated Newton to electric shock therapy, who can blame any person for being afraid to do so? To arrive of the simplest truth, as Newton knew and practiced, requires years of contemplation. Not activity. Not reasoning. Not calculating. Not busy behavior of any kind. Not reading. Not talking. Not making an effort. Not thinking. Simply bearing in mind what it is one needs to know. And yet those with the courage to tread this path to real discovery are not only offered practically no guidance on how to do so, they are actively discouraged and have to set about it in secret, pretending meanwhile to be diligently engaged in the frantic diversions and to conform with the deadening personal opinions that are being continually thrust upon them.

In these circumstances, the discoveries that any person is able to undertake represent the places where, in the face of induced psychosis, he has, by his own faltering and unaided efforts, returned to sanity. Painfully, and even dangerously, maybe. But nonetheless returned, however furtively.

–G. Spencer Brown.*

---

* *The Laws of Form.* London: Geo. Allen & Unwin, 1969.

INTRODUCTION

    This is the story of my personal search of some fifty-six years for meaning in life as we know it. At times in psychoanalytic work, in brain research, in solitude, in interpersonal testing, I have found a thread of truth, of reality, and hence, of meaning. At times the thread has been lost, only to turn up in a new context, in a new place, in a new space, in a new state of consciousness. At other times I have felt the thread to be my own imagined construction – unsharable, idiosyncratic, peculiar to me. At times I have found other persons who independently have found the same or similar threads of truth. These confirmations by others are helpful and precious – otherwise, one is alone and lonely. Without consensus one is unsure, lost.

    I have spent much time in rather unusual, unordinary states, spaces, universes, dimensions, realities – the young Americans call these places "far out." In the far and near East, they are called by a variety of names – the terms "Satori" and "Samadhi" turn up frequently. Not so long ago, before psychedelic agents became useful tools rather than nightmare producers or esoteric secret ingredients, I would not write this book. I had much of the information, but the time had not come for its writing. It seems to me now that the time has arrived. I am ready, and there seems to be a needful audience.

There is a new natural science, even as introduced by William James and currently lead by youngsters such as Charles Tart and Carlos Castaneda. The inner realities are once more receiving the rational exploration and expert scrutiny formerly reserved for the outer realities. The naturalistic approach to our own inner nature is progressing. Robert A. Monroe's *Journeys Out of the Body** is a talented inner naturalist's report on the fauna, flora, geography, and terrain of some of the inner territories. Another such report is Castaneda's *A Separate Reality*.† Some of the methods of this science and its theories are given by Charles T. Tart in his paper, "On the scientific study of states of consciousness: toward an expanded methodology, and the development of state-specific sciences."‡

During the time of the writing of this book, I've discovered several new maps and several new spaces, which I share here. I've also found that I've been in most of the larger spaces described in the Eastern mystical literature, though without their intellectual "baggage" and detailed safeguarding programs. Satori, or Samadhi, or Nirvana, encompasses vast ranges of conscious states far beyond anything describable in words. Each high-level experience convinces one of the vastness of self and of the universe directly perceivable by self.

In this book I speak as one who has been to the highest states of consciousness or of Satori-Samadhi, and as one who has returned to report to those interested. Some who went to these highest levels

---

* Garden City, N.Y.: Doubleday, 1971.

† New York: Simon & Schuster, 1971.

‡ Distributed at the September, 1971, meeting of the Association for Humanistic Psychology, Washington, D.C.

stayed there. Some came back and taught. Some, very few, came back and wrote. Some came back to stay, too awed or frightened or guilty to teach, report, or ever return there. Others, who have not been to these high levels, write and rewrite about them and how to get there. These writings I do not find helpful; I find them distracting. In my own opinion, only those who have been there can help by direct teaching, by example, by writing, and by confirmation. I have found confirmation by others to be helpful on my own trip.

Such experiences as I report are becoming more common, at least among the young persons in the United States. There are probably many older persons who have finally resolved their anti-Satori programming and make it more or less regularly. Many of the younger generation have managed to avoid the anti-Satori programming and live in high positive states most of the time.

It is my firm belief that the experience of higher states of consciousness is necessary for survival of the human species. If we can each experience at least the lower levels of Satori, there is hope that we won't blow up the planet or otherwise eliminate life as we know it. If every person on the planet, especially those in power in the establishments, can eventually reach high levels or states regularly, the planet will be run with relatively simple efficiency and joy. Problems such as pollution, slaughter of other species, overproduction, misuse of natural resources, overpopulation, famine, disease, and war will then be solved by the rational application of realizable means.

The higher states of consciousness and the means of reaching them are an economic asset worth more money than one can currently measure. A corporation that encourages its management and its labor to achieve basic and higher levels of consciousness can show increasing efficiency, harmony, productivity, improved policies, and better public relations within a few months. Once a corporation can achieve "group-unity," it becomes a new kind of establishment entity beyond its former limits.

As Dr. Robert Waelder once pointed out, the Americans have invented the first conscious, successful, nonlethal method of carrying on continuous evolution-revolution of human institutions and ways of life. This evolutionary method is in their private enterprise system, and in their form of government. The next step in the development of further evolution is the achievement of higher group consciousness throughout the United States and then throughout the world. Corporations, as usual, will lead the way; government will follow; the educational system may be the last to adopt the new way.

The old theories about the action of the brain, of the mind, and of the spirit do not seem to be adequate. We need advances in our points of view, in our theories, and in our facts before we can adequately judge the effects of special experiences on individuals and on groups. In this book I present an open-ended, open-minded metatheory of the supraconscious, expanded-awareness states. This work may help in guiding future explorations in these areas. It is hoped that it will serve as a preliminary mapping.

It seems necessary to relate personal experiences with LSD, with solitude-isolation-confinement, with altered states of consciousness, with personal Satori, and with my learning experiences in negative states or spaces. Although at times these reports may seem to be idiosyncratic, in general they are not so unique. Many of the religious and mystical writers report similar experiences (St. John of the Cross, St. Theresa de Avila, Yogananda, Ramakrishna, Ramana

Maharshi, Sri Aurobindo). I feel that concrete examples illustrate the general points in an effective way in this area.

Mystical states, altered states of consciousness, Satori-Samadhi, LSD states, have each tested professionals in their theories on the functioning of the human mind and brain. They have demonstrated the necessity of expanding our current hypotheses to include these states.

In this book, it is assumed that the human brain is a huge biocomputer whose properties are not yet elucidated and not yet understood in full. Interlock between biocomputers in group action also contains unknowns. Certain properties can be specified to a limited extent for some individuals and some groups.

This approach does not presume that everything can be explained. It is not a closed system of thought. For those who can absorb this technique of thinking and make it part of their own intellectual equipment, a large amount of intellectual rubbish can be cleared away. For those who are ready for this approach and who have sufficient self-discipline, use of proper techniques can clarify their thinking, feeling, and physical movement machinery.

This biocomputer view evolved during my own experiences. Experiments were done on myself to test the theory, to change it, to absorb it, to make it part of me, of my own biocomputer. As the theory entered and reprogrammed my thinking-feeling machinery, my life changed rapidly and radically. New inner spaces opened up; new understanding and humor appeared. And a new skepticism of the above facts became prominent. "My own beliefs are unbelievable," says a new metabelief. Quoting from the text:

> *"In the province of the mind, what is believed to be true is true or becomes true, within limits to be found experientially and experimentally. These limits are further beliefs to be transcended. In the province of the mind, there are no limits."*

This is one of the major messages I wish to give you about inner trips, whether by LSD, by meditation, by hypnosis, by Gestalt therapy, by group work, by studies of dreaming, by isolation-solitude-confinement, by whatever means one uses.

This is what the book is about.

J. C. L.
New York
October 1977

Chapter 1
MY FIRST TWO TRIPS: EXPLORING LSD SPACES AND PROJECTIONS

In this chapter, I am speaking to those who have yet to experience the outer-inner spaces, universes, or body trips that others have experienced by whatever means. I introduce spaces by giving a first-hand account for the first time. I show territories that I have explored. Some are found to be blind alleys, some are found to be of help in making progress for oneself.

First of all, I am in a good space. I enjoy telling you about me, about my experiences. I feel here that I am a teacher, a different kind of teacher from those you have had in school, in college and in graduate school and so forth, but still a teacher. I am a different kind of teacher because I have "been there." I haven't gotten it from books. It is not a rehash of the literature. It comes straight from inside me and I do not feel compelled to teach what I know.

I can hear my scientific and medical colleagues objecting to this approach as nonscientific. But those of you who are reading this, looking for help, will know what I mean. Before I had deep and high experiences for the first time, I had spent several years being trained as a psychoanalyst, several years doing work on the neurophysiology of the brain. I had received the usual medical education, and a good basic scientific education at Cal Tech. I had spent a good deal of time in solitude, isolation, and confinement studies on myself. These experiments were done in darkness, total darkness, in total silence, floating in neutral buoyancy in a tank of water. Under these circumstances, "alone with one's God, one has no alibi." In retrospect, this turned out to be the best possible preparation for my first far-out trip.

In the early fifties, I had the opportunity to take LSD, but I didn't take it, because I felt I was not yet ready. By the early sixties, I felt prepared enough and I found an experienced centered guide who loved me enough to conduct the session. During those years, I knew many people who were doing LSD therapy. I knew many people who had been through LSD therapy. I read practically everything that had been published about acid and acid trips.

I give you these facts to show you how careful I have been and also to introduce you to some of the spaces that I went into, in spite of or because of all this preparation.

For my first two trips, I had a sitter, a guide, a helper, someone who was there alone with me during the whole trip. A safe, protected location was carefully selected for the experience. I had realized through the solitude-isolation-confinement work in the tank that such an important step as the first trip in acid must be taken without "interference," such as accidental interruption, intervention, and gossip among colleagues and friends.

As Freud said seventy years ago, in presenting analyses of his own dreams, "At a certain point, one owes discretion to oneself," and I might add, one owes discretion to one's friends. So a lot of what I will say here may sound indiscreet, but I believe we have come a long way since seventy years ago. Today there are more honest, truthful presentations of "inner happenings" than there could have been in Freud's time. His work opened up new honesty spaces.

I try to be as truthful as I can. There may be those who will try to misuse this information, since we do have a national negative program against LSD. However, so many are now in danger that I would prefer to expose myself to some social criticism rather than have further tragedies occur because I didn't speak. My hope here is that those who read this will be more cautious, more informed, and more able if they must go the LSD or other such routes to Satori-Samadhi-Nirvana.

My guide was experienced. She had gone through a long period of many trips on LSD in a therapeutic setting. Her therapy took place in the fifties, when acid was still being explored in the therapeutic milieu by professionals. All her sessions and trips had been taken with professionals present and only pure LSD-25 had been used. In those days, pure lysergic acid diethylamide tartrate was available from the Sandoz, Company in Switzerland. The material was the purest possible, the isolated dextro form of lysergic acid diethylamide tartrate, uncontaminated with other substances. In those days, you knew what you were getting. It was before "street" acid, before dishonest substitutions for acid were made, before fake acid was available. In the language of today, it was "pure Sandoz."

I had known my guide for years, trusted her, respected her experience, and knew that she could carry me through the trip no matter what happened. I knew she cared for me, respected me, and trusted me.

She selected a house in a remote location by the sea. The trip was arranged so there were forty-eight hours in which to carry it out without interruptions and without commitments or responsibilities on my part or hers outside the trip.

We spent a day before the trip working through my hangups, what I wanted to do under acid, what were my goals, where did I want to go. She indicated in depth that I would be in very strange spaces that eventually would become familiar somehow. Later, she indicated that I would probably be moving so fast that I would miss storing some of the experiences but that the important one would be remembered. She had already demonstrated her confidence at being able to handle negative emotion coming from me. She had understanding and insight into what I wanted to do. Finally, she had the capacity to let me have my own trip once it got started.

She agreed, and not only agreed but proposed, that she stay in the background and be my "safety man" and come in only when a suggestion might help me. I did not need nor want a "programmer" who would give specific directions and would try to move me in various directions. I did not want a therapist.

The purpose of that first trip was to experience as many of the possible spaces and effects of acid on me as could be crammed into that session. I wanted to use all my knowledge from my psychoanalysis, science, and from every other source to experience what acid could do. I found later that most of what I knew through experience and experiment was brought to bear, including knowledge of mathematics, logic, biology, medicine, brain mechanisms, and the functioning of the mind; I brought all of myself to that first session.

The session was started in the morning after a good night's sleep. I was thoroughly rested before taking the LSD. I carefully injected 1 cc. containing one hundred micrograms of pure LSD into the muscle of my thigh. Within twenty minutes I moved over into the new and strange LSD spaces.

I stayed centered, conscious, aware, during the whole experience. Within the first ten minutes of moving into these spaces, I suddenly realized that all of my previous training leading up to this point, all of my preparation, had been worth it. I became high and stayed high for eight hours. I felt competent, centered, and able to move through any space that I could conceive of.

Because of my previous training in the isolation tank, I decided not to wear any clothes on this trip. The environment was such that this was the sage and proper thing to do in order to evolve myself. I had lost my hangups about nudity and the necessity of wearing clothes and I wanted to be completely free and comfortable under these special circumstances. My guide had agreed with this and being similarly free of such hangups was also unclad. This freedom allowed me to make certain kinds of breakthroughs by seeing various projections on my body and on hers.

As the LSD began to take effect, I suddenly said in a very loud voice, while pounding on top of a file, "Every psychiatrist, every psychoanalyst should be forced to take LSD in order to know what is over here." What I meant was that anybody who has anything to do with the human mind and its care should be trained in these spaces.

The usual things happened – things that had been well written about in the literature by Aldous Huxley and many others. The sudden enhancement and deepening of all color and form, the transparency of real objects, the apparent living nature of material matter, all appeared immediately.

I started out by looking at a marble-top table and saw the pattern of the marble become alive, plastic, moving. I moved into the pattern and became part of it, living and moving in the pattern of the marble. I became the living marble.

I lay down on the bed between two stereo loudspeakers and went with Beethoven's Ninth Symphony. The music entered into me and programmed me into a deeply religious experience. The whole experience had first been programmed and stored in my very early youth, when I was a member of the Catholic church serving at Mass and believing, with the intense faith of youth, in everything that I was learning in the church.

I moved with the music into Heaven. I saw God on a tall throne as a giant, wise, ancient Man. He was surrounded by angel choruses, cherubim and seraphim, the saints were moving by his throne in a stately procession. I was there in Heaven, worshiping God, worshiping the angels, worshiping the saints in full and complete transport of religious ecstasy.

My guide reported later that I was kneeling on the bed and obviously looking upward into Heaven with my hands in a prayer position. Inside, I was kneeling in Heaven, seeing, feeling and living the whole scene. Later, I found that this all took place during the first two movements and most of the chorus of this symphony. The chorus was that of the angels praising God, worshiping Him. Later, when the soprano voices became too strident and too strong, I came back out of that space and asked that the music be shut off. It was too much at that point and I was exhausted. I had used up my store of energy. I then lay down on the bed and took a short nap.

During the nap, I became recentered back into the space of the room. I awoke and went into the bathroom. I was about to close the door to urinate, when I suddenly saw that one of the hangups of civilization is closing the bathroom door. I started to laugh uproariously at the pure and unadulterated humor of the closed bathroom door. I left the door open and went ahead and peed. My guide asked what the laughter was about. I was now moving off into other places and couldn't even answer the question, so she didn't press it.

I then looked into the mirror at my own face and saw multiple "projections" onto my own face. I first saw myself as I was at that time and then in flashes occurring about one per second I went through my self-images. I went through many, many of my self-images, hundreds of them, some of them very old, dating back to my childhood. Some of them apparently moved forward in time, showing me as I would be at ninety, completely wrinkled, very old, and desiccated. Others showed me when I was sick, blotchy images with purple and other unpleasant colorings on my face. Some of the images were of my idealized self. I appeared as if a god at times. At other times I appeared as if a cripple. The positive and negative flowed into the projections out of my storage banks.

I suddenly saw how one could project, literally project, visual images out of memory. At this point, I decided to use this power and I projected my father's face onto mine, then his father's face. I continued backward in a sequence of new faces that I believed to be my ancestors. Every second a new face appeared.

I pushed back through, I would estimate, two thousand generations and suddenly the face of a hairy anthropoid appeared on my face. My humor came to the fore at this point and I said, "Oh, you can project anything including the Darwinian theory of the origin of Man." I started to laugh, enjoying the spectacle. Suddenly, the face of a sabretooth tiger appeared in the place of mine, with six-inch fangs coming out of his mouth, a very friendly tiger, but nonetheless a so-called dangerous sabretooth.

At this point, I suddenly saw that one had a choice of interpretations here. This could be something dredged out of my unconscious, some threatening thing from the past. Or, it could be my idea of what the anthropoid's dangers were. This could be a racial memory, this could be an imagined thing based on my previous knowledge, or this could just be an event that had no contemporary model to explain it.

Since I was on a high, I thoroughly enjoyed this experience and elaborated it further. I didn't stop to explain to myself what was happening. I watched it happen and as soon as I would think of something new to happen, it did happen. It was a really joyful use of my intellect and knowledge.

I found that I had used up a good deal of my energy and went back on the bed, lay on my back, and closed my eyes. I came back to the present with my guide and then started off on a trip back through memory.

I lived out many of the scenes of my childhood, happy ones, satisfying ones, playing with little playmates, being suckled by mother, being back in the uterus, floating in empty, wonderful, ecstatic space, surrounded by light. I became smaller and smaller in the uterus, going backwards in time until I was the fertilized egg. Suddenly I was two. I was in a sperm; I was in an egg. Time reversed and they suddenly came together. There was a fantastic explosion of joy, of consummation, of completion, as I became one and started to grow back up through all of the embryonic stages. I went through my birth, experiencing the shock of leaving that wonderful safe place, of coming out and being unable to breath, gasping, suffocating with the pressure of the uterus expelling me.

When my guide saw what I was suffering, she understood what I was going through and let me go through it. She said later that I had to re-experience my birth and understand it. She didn't interfere when I started gasping, but she did watch me very carefully. She watched my color and made sure that I wasn't going to push myself too far. As I came through out of the birth canal into the light, I gave a tremendous gasp. All the choking and pushing was over and I was clear. I rested, breathing quietly, feeling all of the new feelings coming from the stimulation of my skin and eyes.

With my guide's cooperation, I relived my first nursing experience. I opened my mouth and something warm came into my mouth from something soft outside, a really beautiful experience. I came back out of that space, into the room again, lying on the bed, smiling happily, peaceful, after all of the storm and drama. My guide described me as looking more peaceful than she had seen me in years.

The trip lasted exactly eight hours, because that was my expectation from the literature. Later I found that my expectation had turned off the acid effect at precisely the expected time. Thus I learned about "self-metaprogramming." In other words, one's own beliefs preprogram to a certain extent what happens when one is under acid.

After 10 years of work in the isolation tank, I had made a generalization from my experiences in the tank. Let me state this as simply as possible. *What one believes to be true, either is true or becomes true in one's mind, within limits to be determined experimentally and experientially. These limits are beliefs to be transcended.* This is the situation when one is freed up from one's environment, from one's surrounding reality, and all of the usual forms and patterns of stimulation are attenuated to the minimum possible level.

In stepping back into ordinary consensus reality, I almost regretted having to leave the LSD space. But I was fatigued by the massive outpouring of energy that had gone on. I seemed to have been operating at ten times my normal speed. Now I needed sleep. That night I slept like a baby for twelve solid hours. I woke up feeling thoroughly alone, integrating and observing what I had been through. "Grokking in fullness waiting is."[*]

It is absolutely essential after such trips to have at least one full day alone, observing what went on and, if possible, writing up or dictating what happened for later reference when one wants to refer back to the first trip.

---

[*] Robert A. Heinlein, Stronger in a Strange Land. New York: G. P. Putnam & Sons, 1961.

This writing or dictating has two major benefits. One, it keeps one oriented during the secondary period, coming after the primary phase of the LSD effect itself. One has about three days to a week after a session in which to absorb it, "to grok it in fullness," to make it part of oneself. Any activities on that second day should be kept to a minimum. There should be no responsibilities or commitments so that one can absorb what happened during the LSD state.

In a sense, an LSD session can be metaphorically called a "pupation" period. The caterpillar forms the cocoon and then proceeds to total reorganization as a pupa. Only after a period of apparent disorganization and reformation can the butterfly form. After the butterfly is formed, it must rest and realize its being as a butterfly. It has moved from a crawling existence to a flying existence and before it can fly, it must become dry, allow its wings to spread and form itself. The LSD session itself is the pupation, the period of organized disorganization, in which things are moving around with a fluidity and a plasticity that one normally does not experience. Unless some direction is put into this process of pupation, one can be uncertain as to how one will come out, still a caterpillar, or some monstrous combination of caterpillar and butterfly, or as a butterfly.

In my experience, the day after the session is quite as important as the session. Directed, self-disciplined movement is necessary on that second day. If one is the sort of person who is willing to do it, it is best to be alone. If not, be with those who have your good will, who have "heart" for you, who believe in you, who want to see you evolve, and who can help you evolve.

Possibly the ideal thing is for the guide to be available when needed that second day in order to discuss points that you may want to discuss. But you still lead during this, the guide does not lead under these circumstances.

The guide can point out, can be a "fair witness"* to you, can give you information about what was happening outside while you were going through these internal spaces. It is useful and sometimes very necessary to know what was happening outside while you were launched into some of these strange spaces.

On the second day, I spent a lot of time free associating and trying to pin down where the experiences had come from. I had heard about the transcendental mystical religious experiences written up in the literature of LSD. I had been skeptical of these as a scientist and an explorer and yet I had gone through one myself. How was I to explain this? How was I to fit this into me and make it part of me? It was apparently a real experience of going to a real heaven and experiencing religious fervor and devotion, something I hadn't experienced for years.

On the second day I was able to go back through memory and get to the period of my childhood when I believed in the Catholic church. Suddenly I began to remember that I had had visions very similar to the experience under LSD when I was a little boy preparing for confession in a darkened church. I was kneeling facing the altar; there was a single candle lighted on the altar and the rest

---

* The "fair witness" is a mode of functioning of the biocomputer in which the self-metaprogrammer remains uninvolved and objective, recording whatever happens without editing or censoring; later, the recording is reproduced on demand exactly, unedited and uncensored. Everyone has a fair witness; some persons must unbury him.

of the church was darkened, with very little light coming in from the outside since the windows were high up. Suddenly the church disappeared, the pillars were shadowy and I saw angels, God on His throne and the saints moving through the church in another set of dimensions. Since I was only seven years old and had seen paintings of artistic concepts of God, this is what I saw in the visions. I also saw His love, His caring, and His creation of us. With this opening up of my memories, which had been repressed during my adult years while pursuing scientific and medical careers, I suddenly saw that what I had gone through with the LSD had been a highly energized, extremely positive experience that somehow had been pushed out of memory in my adult life. I found that I was reluctant to put down the experience. It was recent, highly positive, highly valued, and somehow this apparently was happening as some sort of a lesson to me. Either it was all happening inside my own brain and I was remembering what had happened in childhood or something else was happening, something farther out. Suddenly I realized that I couldn't explain the childhood experience or the LSD experience so patly. Suddenly I was freed from overexplaining anything about this experience. I fully realized that my childhood and my adult experience were practically identical. The experience may have been brought in from memory, and lived through once again because it had been repressed. However there seemed to be more to it than just that.

One could put down the child of seven and say that he had been fed programs of the visions of saints, of Saint Theresa of Avila, that the mystical aspects of the Catholic church had been thoroughly programmed into this young man and that he was projecting his visions totally. I then remembered that I had made the mistake of confiding in a nun that I had had this vision. She was horrified and said that only saints had visions, putting me down thoroughly. At that point I repressed the memory and that kind of experience, but before I repressed it I was angry: "So she doesn't think I'm a saint."

Coming back up to adult life, I laughed when I discovered all of this; I saw that I could project from storage even ecstatic, transcendental mystical and religious experiences. I made a sudden leap forward and realized what a beautiful mechanism we are.

But I was still left with no real explanation, no satisfying explanation for either experience, the first one or the reinvoked one. I tried putting it down in Freudian terms, saying that the first vision was a wishful thinking construction of a childish imagination and that the second one was merely a reliving of the first experience. In one sphere of my thinking this was satisfying. In another it was not.

I had had other experiences four times when I was close to death which had said, "This is not all there is." Continuing my integration and exploration of the second day, I went back into one of the close-to-death experiences. As a Catholic child I was exposed to death. When a relative would die, we had to view the body, attend the funeral, and go through the usual Catholic rituals having to do with death. I was thoroughly acquainted with the concept of the soul leaving the body of the person at the time of death. Also, I had imagined, in the privacy of my own bed as a little boy, my soul taking off and winging toward God and toward Heaven.

This also turned out to be a preparation for that first LSD session when I was listening to Beethoven's Ninth Symphony. I literally left my body and went to Heaven, just as I had wished to do and had done in dream states as a little boy.

I kept reminding myself, "In the province of the mind, what one believes to be true either is true or becomes true within limits to be found experientially." Later I was to realize that the limits of one's beliefs set the limits of the experiences. At the limits of one's creative imagination (whatever that is!), there are a set of beliefs yet to be transcended. The learning process is on a vast scale.

As soon as one learns of one's limits, one can transcend those limits. One's beliefs are then more open and a new set of limits is formed with the new beliefs beyond those. The original beliefs are included as a subset. My mathematical training in set theory began to operate and I realized that where I had been at each stage of my life was determined by my beliefs at that time. Each set of those beliefs became a subset in a bigger set, as I moved on and increased my knowledge and experience. During this second day, I suddenly began to remember things that had happened which I hadn't written up earlier. For example, I remember projecting a face onto my body in the mirror. When one sees this "corporeal" or body face projection, one suddenly realizes that one did this as a child also. If one stands opposite a full length mirror, so that one can see the whole body, one can imagine that there is no real head there in the mirror. The top of the corporeal head is the shoulders, then the nipples become the eyes, the umbilicus or belly button becomes the nose and the pubic hair becomes the mouth. In the male, the penis hanging down is a tongue hanging out of the mouth. In the female, the tongue is inside.

One can project all sorts of things onto this face, once one sees it. It can look like the face of an idiot, if you are on a down trip in regard to your body. It can look like a very happy face if one is content with one's body. It can look like a sexually aroused beast if one is putting down one's sex but is sexually aroused.

When I saw this on my own body, I turned and looked at my guide and saw it on her body. The eyes that were popping out were the female breasts, and the tongue was missing from the mouth. As I watched, she suddenly became a golden goddess, a fantastic beauty.

As I felt the excitement and longing with that picture, suddenly it shifted, the emotion changed to fright and panic and she became a female ravening gorilla covered with hair, and dripping from her genitals with mad sexual desire of a bestial sort. My guide saw my fright and saw that I was projecting something from my dark negative part onto her. When I told her that I was projecting the female ravening gorilla, I had tuned in on a very dark part of her, and she had identified with my projection.

She had reacted to my projection with her own hangup in this area and had let me have it. She had been taken in on my trip, and reflected my own emotion with anger that I should project onto her whom I loved such a horrifying image.

We started the "two-mirror oscillation effect," each projecting on the other and each further projection causing the other to appear with negative enhancement. I learned that one had to deal with the hangups in one's guide as well as one's own hangups.

I had to come back out of the LSD state and deal with my guide's upset at that point. I reminded her that this was my projection, not hers, and that she had agreed not to get involved in my trip. A lot of emotional tension developed between us.

She quickly came out of this negative state as I described the other image I had projected on her. We then discussed this polarity in my view of women. Because of my childhood religious training, I pictured women as either remote goddesses or angels with no sex whatsoever, or dangerous, sexually seductive animals.

This split in my view of women was so obvious at that point that, on the second day, I had to spend a lot of time working that one through. I finally associated it with women who had been in my life.

I had started out by projecting a goddess image on my women, making them more than they possibly could be, or anybody could be, in terms of purity, virtue, and all of the positive qualities. Later having accomplished the sexual act with them and having experienced orgasm with them, having experienced their orgasms, I demeaned them as having given in to their animal nature. This was straight from the teaching of the Catholic church. Again, it was a projection into real situations brought forward in time from my past.

I had been taught that sexual impulses, anger, and so on, were part of one's animal nature and were sinful. "Carnal desires" were to be put down, controlled, in order that one could become a saint. This split had taken place quite early in my life, and I was still carrying it around at the time of the first LSD session, in spite of a lot of analytic work. The analytic work that I had done in my psychoanalysis with Robert Waelder had uncovered enough material so I would see this split in action during my first experience with LSD. Probably I wouldn't have had such freedom without that analysis and I might have identified with the negative projections and had a bum trip.

I could freely experience the poles of my desires and idealism and the poles of my fright and horror because of this preparation. For the first time, I was able to see the extremely positive pole and the extremely negative pole, between which my life oscillated. In regard to women I had oscillated between the goddess and the gorilla. Obviously I had sexual hangups to be worked on. I had ideals out of consonance with reality and I had fear-filled spaces within me, centering around sex, aggression, and threat. Later I was to find the bipolar nature of the dichotomies in many other areas of my existence, my being, and my knowledge. I felt after this review session that I could understand something of the "beyond good and evil" concept. My Fair Witness was developing. Each of us has within us a "Fair Witness" observer that faithfully and objectively perceives and records what is really happening.

I was still on a high that second day, and the high went on for a period of two weeks. As a result of this prolonged high, I made another mistake. In the euphoria of these "tremendous discoveries" and with the overwhelming self-confidence resulting therefrom, I was led into one of the LSD traps.

I felt that I had mastered the knowledge gained during the LSD experience, but as it turned out, I had not mastered this knowledge. There was still more bad material to go through, still more nonsense programs in me to be brought to light.

After this trip, this session, I took a real trip to Hawaii for the first time. I spent ten days in Hawaii, continuing on the high, and sharing my newfound knowledge with my friends in Hawaii. The experience of the tropical islands enhanced the high. I came back all ready for a second trip, thinking that the high would continue and that I could stay that way permanently.

I undertook my second trip with the same guide in another location, two weeks after the first trip. The circumstances were not so favorable as for the first experience. After the second session, I was due to return home to an unhappy family situation. This dominated the second session. I spent the second session preoccupied with my problems with my wife. I walked up and down the room first berating her, then berating myself, trying to reform her personality along more ideal lines. Seeing how I, too, did not come up to my ideals, I came down off my high during this trip and got into some very sticky areas, having to do with my performance in my two marriages and my lack of integration of a family life with my professional life.

Thus I learned that expectations also lead to programming of sessions. Where you are going after the session, what you are going to be doing then, can preprogram the session to the point where you live out certain expectations. Under these circumstances, you can go on a really bum trip. I worked through a good deal of very personal material, having to do with my wife and child, and my previous wife and her children, and came to no solution of the real situation existing. No matter what I would imagine or any theory that I would construct, the facts of existence as I saw them could not be changed. In addition I was under pressure of the preprogramming of a scheduled talk to a scientific society across the continent.

The second session did not take place with the relaxed atmosphere of the first one. I was under pressure and it came out in the session. I was so preoccupied with these matters and with talking to myself out loud into a tape recorder about them, that my guide lost contact with me, went out into the other room, and left me to work out my own destiny. I did not go into any far-out internal spaces this trip. I stayed with the current problem and discussed it with myself and hallucinated real persons, getting them to give their side, and I gave my side to them. I came out of that session feeling rather hopeless about my marriage, about any possibility of changing my wife's mind or her personality or her knowledge.

I did not have time to integrate the LSD experiences, to recapitulate and "grok in fullness," that I had had in the first session, because the next day I flew across the continent. That night I gave the speech to a scientific society. After I had finished the speech, I left the banquet room and pushed the elevator button to go up to my room in the hotel. That's the last thing I remembered until I became conscious three days later in a hospital in that city.

In the meantime, I almost died. I had been in a coma for approximately twenty-four hours, and had been blind for two days. I literally didn't know what had happened for a week. I lay in that hospital bed trying to figure out how I had got there. I could remember giving the speech, pushing the button of the elevator, and from that point on there was a complete blackout as to what had happened. I could remember something about LSD, I could remember everything that happened up to the point of pushing that button, so I knew I had my work cut out for me. Until my vision came back, I was in no shape to analyze or attempt to remember. I was fighting for my life, for my vision, for my whole future. After my vision returned and I was able to see, I then had time, six weeks of convalescence time, to recapitulate, to remember, to piece together what had happened to me.

Once again, during that time, I was able to see that I had gone through another close-to-death experience. Without the expert medical and neurological care that I had received at the hands of my medical colleagues and friends, I would not be here today. My life was saved by the lucky happenstance of a friend finding me in that hotel room and getting me to a hospital where I was known, and where there was a high level of neurological and brain competence.

Chapter 2

NEAR-LETHAL "ACCIDENT":
"NO EXPERIMENT IS A FAILURE"

In the use and misuse of LSD one must be aware that if one has programs that are self-destructive, one must be extremely careful to have proper guidance and proper advice before, during, and after sessions. Because of the releasing quality of the "pupation" period caused by LSD, programs below levels of awareness are released. In the usual state of consciousness there are counterprograms working against those that are deadly. In the LSD state, the connections between these programs, which insure survival of the organism, are loosened.

During my second LSD session, a good deal of grief, anger, and guilt had been released. I had succeeded in breaking my emotional bonds with my wife during that session. This caused the release of a deadly program, though I was not aware of this until after I gave the speech and pushed the elevator button.

In the weeks after being released from the hospital, I was able to reconstitute the amnesic period and recover what had happened. Apparently I had gone to my hotel room, extremely lonely and grief-stricken, filled with guilt and in the grips of a program, which I didn't recognize. The LSD session had loosened a lot of my defenses against this particular program.

I am reluctant to go into the details of this episode because, as Freud said, "One owes discretion to oneself (and one's friends) at some point." I will give the biological organic details without all of the personal psychological meanings to illustrate how "an accident" can be caused by a stored program taking over.

While giving myself an antibiotic shot, "by accident" I injected under my skin a foam made with a detergent. The syringe had residual detergent in it which I failed to clean out. Somehow the bubbles had gotten into my circulation, passed through the lungs, and had lodged in my brain, cutting off the circulation to very critical parts of my brain, including the visual cortex. I had then gone into immediate coma. Later I struggled up from the depths of the coma, got to the telephone in the room, and called the operator who then sent up the house detective. I went into coma again. When the detective arrived, he asked me for the name of a friend in the hotel. With great effort I could think only of a neurologist in Chicago at that point. Meanwhile my head was pounding and I thought that I had blown a blood vessel in my brain. The pain was the most excruciating that I have ever experienced. I went into coma again, struggled back out of coma, and named a friend who was in the hotel. He said later that when he arrived in the room, I was in coma and it took him six hours to get an ambulance. Meanwhile, I was lying there on the hotel bed. I remember very well the inside experience that occurred while I was in the so-called coma.

The pounding headache, the nausea and the vomiting that occurred forced me to leave my body. I became a focused center of consciousness and traveled into other spaces and met other beings, entities, or consciousnesses. I came across two who approached me through a large empty space and who looked, felt, and transmitted guiding and teaching thoughts to me. It is very hard to put this experience into words, because there were no words exchanged. Pure thought and feeling was being transmitted and received by me and by these two entities. I will attempt to translate into words what occurred. I am in a large empty place with nothing in any direction except light. There is a golden light permeating the whole space everywhere in all directions, out to infinity. I am a single point of consciousness, of feeling, of knowledge. I know that I am. That is all. It is a very peaceful, awesome, and reverential space that I am in. I have no body, I have no need for a body. There is no body. I am just I. Complete with love, warmth, and radiance.

Suddenly in the distance appear two similar points of consciousness, sources of radiance, of love, of warmth, I feel their presence, I see their presence, without eyes, without a body. I know they are there, so they are there. As they move toward me, I feel more and more of each of them, interpenetrating my very being. They transmit comforting, reverential, awesome thoughts. I realize that they are beings far greater than I. They begin to teach me. They tell me I can stay in this place, that I have left my body, but that I can return to it if I wish. They then show me what would happen if I left my body back there – an alternative path for me to take. They also show me where I can go if I stay in this place. They tell me that it is not yet time for me to leave my body permanently, that I still have an option to go back to it. They give me total and absolute confidence, total certitude in the truth of my being in this state. I know with absolute certainty that they exist. I have no doubts. There is no longer any need for an act of faith; it just is that way and I accept it.

Their magnificent deep powerful love overwhelms me to a certain extent, but I finally accept it. As they move closer, I find less and less of me and more and more of them in my being. They stop at a critical distance and say to me that at this time I have developed only to the point where I can stand their presence at this particular distance. If they come any closer, they would overwhelm me, and I would lose myself as a cognitive entity, merging with them. They further say that I separated them into two, because that is my way of perceiving them, but that in reality they are one in the space in which I found myself. They say that I insist on still being an individual, forcing a projection onto them, as if they were two. They further communicate to me that if I go back to my body as I developed further, I eventually would perceive the oneness of them and of me, and of many others.

They say that they are my guardians, that they have been with me before at critical times and that in fact they are with me always, but that I am not usually in a state to perceive them. I am in a state to perceive them when I am close to the death of the body. In this state, there is no time. There is an immediate perception of the past, present, and future as if in the present moment.

I stayed in this state for many hours in earth time. Then I came back to my body in the hospital. I had another pain in my head and came out of the coma to find that they were injecting something into my carotid arteries in the neck. I immediately perceived that they were looking for a brain lesion, for bleeding into the brain, by injecting a radio-opaque substance for X-rays. Once the pain was exhausted, I went back into coma, returning to the two guardians.

The next time that I returned to my body and awoke, I was in a hospital room. The pain in my head was gone, but I could not see.

There was a brilliant white sheet of light, immediately in front of my eyes, filling my whole visual field. I could feel my body and move the various parts. I found I was not paralyzed. I found that I could talk and that I could think clearly, so I realized the brain damage was not as extensive as I had feared. I thought, "The guardians are right. I can stay in my body, but blind."

I went through an intense grief reaction to having come back to a blind body, but I trusted the guardians' "statement" that I would be all right. I lay in the hospital bed, reviewing my knowledge of neurology and of brain mechanisms. I figured out that I was blind because of an irritative rather than a destructive lesion in my visual cortex. The guardians were right. I must wait and see how much of my vision was left when the irritation stopped, when the blinding white light was turned off.

When the doctors came in and found me awake, we discussed my case. I still didn't know what had happened. I knew who I was and when they told me where I was, I recognized the hospital.

An ophthalmologist examined my eyegrounds. He said that there was no visible lesion in my eyes. This relieved me very much. The irritation was not in the retina; it was in the brain. If it had been in the retina, there would be less hope for recovery.

During the period of the great white light in front of my eyes, I experienced some new phenomena. First of all, I couldn't see any light in the room, whether it was day or night. The inside light was so bright that it made no difference at all what sort of patterns were coming into my eyes. When the ophthalmologist examined my eyes, I couldn't see his light, which was very bright. My "central seeing computer" was firing so strongly that outside stimulation coming in through the eyes could not influence the result. The inside observer was blinded only because the information coming to him (wherever he is) from the visual cortex was so strong that any added stimulation from the periphery made no difference. All lines were busy all the time. This showed me that the observing systems in my large computer were not in the irritated visual cortex itself. I studied the great white light; I began to see new phenomena. As I lay on the bed in the hospital, various kinds of visions occurred.

Suddenly I saw a green lawn, but the grass looked totally artificial as if made out of plastic. On this lawn there was a hole, out of which a snake came. The snake rose out of the hole straight into the air. Suddenly I laughed because he was such an artificial man-made snake. The snake was constructed with a spring down his center and he was covered with paper. His head was made out of painted wood. His jaws were articulated around a single nail. Coming in from the right was a wooden bird, brilliantly painted, flapping his wooden wings and opening and closing his wooden beak. The snake rose up and bit the wooden bird with his wooden jaws.

This whole episode occurred while I was in a very relaxed state, just watching it happen. I remembered that, as a very small boy, I had a wooden snake and a wooden bird just like this. I suddenly realized that part of my memory storage system was firing and transmitting these pictures into the "visual display" part of my computer. As soon as I realized that this was a memory elaborated by my child's imagination, I began to laugh. As soon as I laughed, it disappeared. I then relaxed and various other animals made out of wood appeared. When I was two to three years old, I had had a wooden Noah's Ark. The animals became animated, moving about across the artificial grass. One characteristic of all these movements was the hesitancy and the wobbliness of the movements, as if the child were imagining these animals, making them move. The child was creating this movement in his imagination and not doing too good a job of it. This characteristic wobbliness of the construction is apparently a property of the child brain of a much earlier time.

Slowly during the next forty-eight hours, the brilliance of the white light decreased. The childish visions disappeared and in their place, there was a swarm of insect like points of light and darkness which moved across the visual field. I found I could program their direction of flight and their speed. When I thought they would move in a particular direction, later the swarm moved in that direction.

My programming was ahead of what happened. I could think "now they will move to the right," and within a few seconds, they moved to the right. One puts a program into the computer; the computer then executes the program and generates the result with a delay between the time of the intent and the time of the carrying out of the result. I found later that for a very complex program this process can take up to three to four minutes; with the swarms of insect-like points, the delay was a few seconds.

When the neurologist in charge came in during this period, I told him something of these visual displays I was seeing. He said, "Oh, you're hallucinating. Would you like to see a psychiatrist?" My reply was, "Please, this is not a psychiatric matter. This will give us information about what parts of the brain have been irritated." I thought to myself, "I should call one of my French neurological friends who understands the production of visual displays by irritation of various parts of the brain."

This old tendency of medical people to attribute hallucinations only to mentally ill persons and to put down visual displays as "hallucinations" has bothered me for some years.

I learned my lesson, however, and didn't speak of these matters any further with any of the attending staff.

The brilliant white light decreased in intensity, and after eighteen hours, I was to the point where stimulation from the eyes could come through to me. The first time that I could see was in the middle of the night when a nurse came in to give me an injection. There was a single light on in the room and through the fog of the remaining residual internal white light, I saw two round black circles and a foggy face behind them. I was looking at the face of the nurse and I said to her, laughing with relief, "You look just like an owl."

She said, "You see now." I said "Yes" and she went out and asked one of the doctors to come in to check my eyes. Within the next twenty-four hours my vision came back, almost totally intact.

There were only two little spots below my fixation point, one in each eye, which didn't come back. Subsequent tests outlined these two missing places in my visual field. They turned out to be very small. The attending ophthalmologist said that they might recover during the next few weeks. This turned out not to be the case and over the subsequent years these two spots have remained to continuously remind me of the dangers that one can get into with this kind of experimentation. Even today, five years later, I have difficulty in reading columns of figures. The spots are below the points of fixation; I do not see the figures coming up when I read vertically. However, I can read horizontally quite easily.

I was told to convalesce for the next six weeks, not to do a lot of reading and to let my nervous system totally recover. A friend allowed me to stay at his house for some time. I went into the country and spent the next six weeks recovering my strength. During this period of convalescence, I analyzed what had happened. I recovered most of my memories and rebuilt myself, my view of myself, and my view of where I wanted to go.

It turned out that the experience with the guardians was the fourth time that I had gone to that place. I had left my body three times before, each time under a threat of death.

The first time that I can remember was when I was seven years old and I was having my tonsils removed under ether. I was extremely frightened as I went under the ether and I immediately found myself in a place with two angels who folded their wings around me and comforted me. The angel form was the childish projection onto the entities necessary to a child of seven brought up in the Catholic church.

The second time was when I was ten years old and had some disease, possibly tuberculosis, which made me very debilitated. I was in bed for six weeks or more. I used to wander off into this region when the room was quiet and nobody was present, when I had a high fever.

The third time was when I was twenty-two years old, having four wisdom teeth removed under a local anesthetic. I became very frightened as the dentist had a chisel pointed right at my brain. The pain of it and the imaginary catastrophe of having that chisel slip and go into my brain put me into primary shock. I sweated and became white and nauseated. The dentist saw this and gave me nitrous oxide.

Under nitrous oxide I went into a whirling space, a total experience of everything whirling. Sound, light, my body, the whole universe was whirling. I moved from that space suddenly into the space with the two guardians. At that time they instructed me as to what I was going to be doing, or what I should do, and hadn't yet done. When I came back out of the nitrous oxide, my teeth had been pulled and I felt a huge and immense relief. Now I knew where I was going and what I was going to do. That was when I decided to go to medical school and learn more about the survival of myself and others.

These memories, which were brought back during this long period of self-analysis after the accident, showed me the continuity of this space, of these two guardians. I realized that this is a place that I can go to and that presumably other people can go to, under special circumstances. During those weeks I resolved to get back to that place and to try to do it without the threat of death. I thought of deep trance states and of using LSD to achieve this level of consciousness.

I also reconstructed how the "accident" had occurred. I remembered that during World War II, when I was doing research on bends (the formation, at high altitudes, of bubbles that are released into the blood), I discovered that a foam, made of a detergent, could be lethal.

At the time we were trying to find the pathways that bubbles took from the legs into the lungs. I injected foam into the leg vein of a dog and found that it went through the lungs into the brain. The detergent bubbles lowered the surface tension to the point where the bubbles could slip through the small capillaries of the lungs, go to the brain, and lodge there in the capillaries of the brain.

With the bends, most of the bubbles were trapped in the lungs and caused a syndrome called "chokes," in which the subject began to feel tickling sensations in the chest, began to cough and suddenly became very blue as the flow of blood through the lungs was stalled. The cure for chokes was merely to increase the pressure around the subject to the point where the bubbles collapsed. In the high altitude chamber, we did "crash dives" to atmosphere in order to collapse the bubbles.

The important point is that the information had been stored in me 20 years before. I had "forgotten" that this information was there. In the throes of the grief and the guilt released by the second LSD session, I had apparently injected the foam; something in me knew that this was a lethal act. The most frightening thing about this whole episode was the fact that part of me could use information stored in me to kill the rest of me. Insofar as I could remember, I was not consciously trying to commit suicide. At the time, it was literally an "accident."

When I realized that I had such lethal programs stored within me that they could destroy me if I gave in to them or if I wasn't aware of their presence, I decided to do a much more thorough self-analysis and root out these programs.

My analyst had warned me that such destructive tendencies existed. Apparently he was aware, even though I wasn't.

In fact, I had become so frightened before this episode that I had called my analyst and made an appointment to see him on the very day that this accident happened. After my self-examination and the six weeks of convalescence, I paid him a visit and spent two hours working on this problem. I told him what I could remember and, through free association with him, recovered more of the memories. The only reason that I am relating all of this very personal material is to illustrate the general principle:

> *There can exist, in addition to the aware self, other hidden systems of control of the organism, which can program thinking, can program feeling, can program action, toward destruction of that particular organism. LSD can release these programs, can strengthen them, and can weaken the aware surviving self to the point where there is danger of suicide or of self-destructive activities.*

Therefore, examine yourself very carefully. Do a very critical self-examination and get help from someone else who knows you very well. If you have any hint of such programs, be sure that you place all the safeguards possible around yourself, to prevent these programs from being activated under LSD to the point where you endanger your own body.

My mistake was two LSD sessions too close together without adequate preparation for analysis between the two sessions and after the second session. The fact that I had to give the talk broke up the self-analysis period for the second session. Possibly, if I had been able to carry out the analysis during a week following the second session I might have been able to avoid this almost fatal episode.

I suspect that these programs have been released in those cases in which the person under LSD ends up walking off the balcony or in front of a car. I do not think it is because of illusions or delusions projected onto the outside world as much as it is a release of the self-destructive programs. During periods of intense emotion which can be released by techniques discussed later as well as by LSD, such programs can be activated and can gain control of the whole system.

Thus, included among the maps and the mapping of maps needed for successful navigation in the inner spaces with any method as well as with LSD are destructive programs. It is wise to explore these danger areas, not to repress them. Explore them carefully and with the proper help. One needs a guide in these areas who knows one very well and who can give one some understanding of them, thus preventing these destructive programs from taking over.

I had no such guide and didn't use the one that was available. During the second session, my guide had left me. I had gone into these negative spaces without someone else to monitor me and to put me straight and to show me that I had activated these lethal systems. I had sensed that I should get to my analyst, but the episode occurred before I was able to make it.

During the design of subsequent experiments with LSD, I made sure that a good solid person, well grounded and well centered, was available immediately in the environment of the experience. Any time any of this kind of negative thinking happened, I could go to that person and straighten it out before it got to the point where I could not control it.

I had learned many lessons from this episode and, as it is said in scientific circles, "No experiment is a failure." I had learned that death is not as terrifying as I had imagined it to be, that there is another space, a safe place beyond where we are now. Instead of being frightened off from further experimentation, I became intrigued and decided to explore this very region.

I set up experiments using LSD in the solitude, isolation, and confinement tank, floating in the darkness, and silence, freed of all inputs to my body from the external reality. In these experiments, I discovered other spaces, found other maps, and discovered relatively safe means of going into these places without having the lethal programs activated too strongly again.

Luckily my role as an explorer had not been endangered but had been strengthened by this lesson. I say "luckily" because I did survive. I no longer feared the ultimate consequences of the negative programs. My fear of death or of leaving this body diminished. I had also discovered that my mission was to do exploring in this region. This meant that I must clean up my life and fit myself further for continuing this work.

This episode led to trouble with my professional reputation as a scientist. The rumor went around that the episode had happened as a result of taking LSD at the time and that LSD had damaged my brain. LSD was found in my briefcase in the hospital. Immediately the medical people attributed the whole episode to my having taken LSD in the hotel.

This was wrong. The rumor that my brain had been damaged was reversed when I later went for a neurological examination and it was found that I was quite intact. I counted the number of ampoules of LSD present and was convinced that I had not used any in the hotel. There were 6 ampoules in the beginning, a full box, before the two LSD sessions, and there were 4 left.

Insofar as I am able, I have given the facts and the lessons learned. Take this lesson for your own. Reread the account, put yourself through it as if you were me, absorb it, "grok in fullness." It may serve to get you through a tough place on a bum trip some day.

Chapter 3
RETURN TO THE TWO GUIDES: TANK PLUS LSD

At times one hears rumors that there is a great man, a guru, a master, available, running a school in which one can evolve oneself to new higher levels. One hears of a far-out guru in India somewhere in the Himalayas who has set up a school to teach one how to achieve Samadhi, a state of total consciousness and a state in tune with universal mind. Or one may hear rumors about a Sufi school teaching the traditional esoteric doctrines and exercises of the Sufis. Or one may hear of the latest therapeutic school devised by Dr. So-and-So with his new approach to therapy. At times friends seem to bombard one with the newest information about the latest master, guru, or therapist. What are the aims of these schools? Where do people want to go who join these schools?

In my own mappings of these areas of human endeavor, in my own explorations, I have come across a number of people who have been exposed to such gurus, or masters. I have been impressed by what they have learned and how far they have evolved with this kind of help. I have also been impressed with how publicly they acclaim their guru or master and how much positive transference, as is said in Freudian terms, has developed. This state they are in reminds me very much of the hyperenthusiastic state of some who have taken their first few trips on LSD. They feel they now have the answers to self-evolution. They are now much happier. They now feel much more effective. They radiate warmth and love and concern for others.

At this time this does not seem to be my path. I prefer understanding rather than devotion. I prefer fellow seekers rather than charismatic disciples. I prefer staying in my own center, grounded, and helping others to become centered and grounded rather than developing a group that worships me. In the past I had periods in which I wanted to develop my personal charisma in order to influence others. This now seems to be a nonrealistic, nonefficient method of transmitting knowledge and understanding. One can operate much more effectively by being what one is, rather than by using powers of seduction and persuasion to foster the delusion of being a "great man."

Instead of being a Pied Piper, I would prefer to be an effective teacher of those persons who seek to understand what it is that I have to teach. The Pied Piper entrances and entrains the children of the town and carries them off after him to Lord knows what sort of mission. When these children return, what do they do? They do not have the knowledge, they do not have the understanding, they are not centered and grounded to the extent required to get on with the world's work. They do have stars in their eyes, they do have charisma. They can involve lots of people in their projects, but are their projects worth pursuing?

Yes, there are serious esoteric schools. Yes, there are effective gurus. My bet is that they are doing their work without all of the fanfare and without taking on disciples who shout their names from the housetops. Obviously these schools would not be available to just anyone, they would have "cover stories" for their actual operations. Otherwise they could not operate. They would be overwhelmed by hyperenthusiastic potential disciples. They would have faced long ago the problem of selection of students – the careful selection without fanfare, without publicity.

Without a direct contact with such a school, let us set up what we can hope such a school would do. This of itself can be a helpful exercise in mapping your own inner spaces. Let us imagine what it would be like to have the kind of help that one would like to have in order to move to higher levels of functioning. I have found such metaprogramming to be a help in my own evolution.

Once again I will quote: "What one believes to be true either is true or becomes true within limits to be found experientially and experimentally. These limits are beliefs to be transcended."

In my own far-out experiences in the isolation tank with LSD and in my close brushes with death I have come upon the two guides. These two guides may be two aspects of my own functioning at the supraself level. They may be entities in other spaces, other universes than our consensus reality. They may be helpful constructs, helpful concepts that I use for my own future evolution. They may be representatives of an esoteric hidden school. They may be concepts functioning in my own human biocomputer at the supraspecies level. They may be members of a civilization a hundred thousand years or so ahead of ours. They may be a tuning in on two networks of communication of a civilization way beyond ours, which is radiating information throughout the galaxy.

Whichever of these alternatives seems right to you, it is essential to have something, someone, ahead of one setting the goals of where you are going.

With such knowledge, with such conceptions, with such imaginings, one can, as it were, lift oneself with one's own bootstraps beyond where one is now. If one can believe that one can tune in on help greater than oneself by one's own efforts, it is a great lesson. In other words, one has help in order to transcend one's current limiting beliefs. This belief is of help in the transcendence.

In my own case I had not trusted a human master, a guru, or any human guides. Early in my childhood I was doublecrossed, as it were, by priests, nuns, and others who pretended to have all of the knowledge and the direct contact with God. I became skeptical while quite young. I found more honest truth within myself than I ever did from the representatives of the church. This skepticism led me away from the mystical aspects of the church into science and medical research in the search for new knowledge.

I am sure that if I came across an authentic person who definitely could demonstrate that he had the powers he claimed, I would remain skeptical until it was definitely shown that I could learn what he knew and reach the same places, the same spaces. Meanwhile I pursue my own path in my own inner spaces, skeptical of any help that is not of the above variety. I have seen too much of sham pretension and showmanship in myself and in others to believe in instant enlightenment through contact with a master or guru.

I will illustrate some of the kinds of experiences that are claimed by the esoteric schools by describing some of my own trips in the solitude-isolation tank situation with and without LSD. In these experiences I came across what one might call "supraself" and "supraspecies metaprogrammers," which seemed to me to be outside myself, not embedded in me. Using other languages, other terminologies, one could call these celestial gurus, or divine teachers or guardians. I also got into spaces where the energies and the forces were so vast that there was no humanly conceivable way of transmitting these experiences in words in a book.

The most definite of these experiences was done with LSD in the solitude-isolation-confinement tank. But first let me review the purpose of the original experiments that were done with the tank.

When I was at the National Institute of Mental Health in Bethesda, Maryland, in 1954, working on the neurophysiology of the brain, I conceived of a new set of experiments.

In brief, previous neurophysiologists, including Professor Frederic Bremer of Brussels and Dr. Horace Magoun of UCLA, had hypothesized that the brain stayed in a waking state because of external stimulation coming through the end organs of the body. In other words, outside stimulation was necessary in order to maintain the brain in an awakened state. The obvious experiment was to isolate the human from all external stimulation insofar as this was physically possible, and to see what the resulting states were.

I decided that the way to do it was to float in water using a head-mask in order to breathe and to be in neutral buoyancy within the water so as to attenuate gravity effects. At the same time all sound was to be cut off from the person suspended in the water, all temperature differences over the body were to be attenuated as far as possible, all light was to be cut off, and all stimulating clothing was to be removed.

By coincidence there was a tank already installed at NIH in a small building inside a soundproof room. The only changes I had to make were to put a temperature control valve on the water flow through the tank and to maintain the temperature at 93° F. I did a good deal of experimentation to find this particular temperature. This is the temperature at which one is neither hot nor cold when resting. It is the temperature at which the water disappeared when I didn't move. The resulting sensation was as if one were floating in space almost free of gravity.

Since I had studied human respiration and oxygen masks during World War II, I knew something of the requirements of the breathing system. I worked the technical details out quite satisfactorily. I tried fifteen or twenty different kinds of underwater masks, furnished by the Navy, and found none of them comfortable enough. Therefore it was necessary to devise my own mask out of latex rubber, which covered the whole head and sealed around the neck. There were two breathing tubes going to special valves at the side of the tank to allow continuous supplies of air to reach me and to receive the expired air which left my lungs without allowing the accumulation of carbon dioxide and without causing the depletion of oxygen in the system.

I quickly found that my body had different densities, that my legs and my head tended to sink. This meant devising supports from an extremely smooth fine rubber dam used in surgery to maintain my foot position in the tank without touching the bottom. The head balance was adjusted by allowing a certain amount of air to be in the head mask. After a good deal of such technical matters, I was finally able to reach a state of suspended neutral buoyancy just below the surface of the water in the tank.

Later, such experiences and experiments were called "sensory deprivation." At no time did I find any deprivation effect. In the absence of all stimulation it was found that one quickly makes up for this by an extremely heightened awareness and increasing sensory experience in the absence of known means of external stimulation. Within the first few hours it was found that I did not tend to go to sleep at all. The original theory was wrong. One did not need external stimulation to stay awake. After a few tens of hours of experiences, I found phenomena that had been previously described in various literatures. I went through dreamlike states, trancelike states, mystical states. In all of these states, I was totally intact, centered, and there. At no time did I lose conscious awareness of the facts of the experiment. Some part of me always knew that I was suspended in water in a tank in the dark and in the silence.

I went through experiences in which other people apparently joined me in this dark silent environment. I could actually see them, feel them, and hear them. At other times, I went through dreamlike sequences, waking dreams as they are now called, in which I watched what was happening. At other times I apparently tuned in on networks of communication that are normally below our levels of awareness, networks of civilizations way beyond ours. I did hours of work on my own hindrances to understanding myself, on my life situation. I did hours of meditation, concentration, and contemplation, without knowing that this was what I was doing. It was only later in reading the literature that I found that the states that I was getting into resembled those attained by other techniques.

In 1958, I left the National Institutes of Health and moved to the Virgin Islands. It wasn't until 1964 that I was able to build another tank and to introduce LSD into the solitude isolation and confinement experiment. I quickly discovered that the use of the mask was not necessary with LSD. Since sea water was available, I used this and found that I could float at the surface with mouth and nose and eyes out of the sea water. I found that I could float with my hands holding one another underneath my neck, elbows out to the side underwater. I let my legs dangle from the knees and the hips in the salt water. This procedure of increasing the density of the water allowed a much more simplified breathing system and a greater feeling of safety. This second tank was 8 feet deep and 8 feet on the side. This allowed a lot more space than in the previous tank at NIH. Once the tank was set up and operating with the proper temperature control systems, sufficient air, and a complete blackout of the room, I set about obtaining the LSD.

Through the cooperation of professional colleagues, I found at that time it was legal to obtain LSD if one had a grant from the National Institute of Mental Health. Since I had a Career Award grant which was to run five years, I was able to obtain the LSD directly from the Sandoz Company through the proper channels. I proposed trying LSD on dolphins as an aid to my understanding of the substance and some of the physiological dangers of its use. The only relevance of these experiments to the present account is that I quickly found that there was no danger to breathing in water-suspended mammals. Each of the six dolphins tested apparently had very good trips with no problems attendant upon their breathing, heart action, or swimming activities. These experiments gave me confidence to go ahead and try it on myself.

Insofar as I could find out from the literature, there was no published record of anyone having taken LSD alone, much less under such severe conditions of physical isolation. I remembered memoranda from the early fifties distributed at the NIMH warning people not to take it alone and giving a detailed case history of someone who had tried it alone and became paranoid. He had gone through an experience in which the tape recorder which he was running to record his impressions had tried to eat him.

This was a bad preprogramming for what I intended to do. I had to work through my own fears in regard to doing this alone. I obtained help from a "safety man" who was able to keep all accidental intruders into the experiments away from the laboratory. No one was allowed into the laboratory while the experiments were going on. Over the next two years I was able to do twenty good experiments.

This series was terminated by the national negative program which started in 1966 against LSD. Such work was no longer to be done under the new regulations and the new laws. Each investigator was asked to return his LSD to the Sandoz Company at that time, which I did.

As I said above, I had a lot of fear with regard to the first experience. Previously I had had two trips with a guide. I had had a close brush with death and therefore had a profound respect for those programs below levels of awareness that could deal lethal blows to oneself. In addition, I had gotten over my fear of death. It wasn't bodily death that I feared; it was getting into spaces in which I would lose control and from which I would perhaps not be able to come back. In other words, it was more a fear of psychosis than of death that was motivating me at this time.

In spite of these doubts and fears, however, I took 100 micro grams and got into the tank. In the first experience, I devoted most of my time to devising a basic belief structure that would make future experiments safer. I spent about an hour in the tank working on whether or not my heart and respiration would continue if I did leave my body. I quickly learned that under LSD, if one can relax and enjoy it, one's heart and respiration do become automatic and one does not have to worry about them. I also learned that by holding my hands under the back of my neck and putting my arms out sideways there was no danger of tipping over in the tank. I learned also that if one does tip over or if one puts one's head back too far, the salt seawater getting into one's eyes or nose quickly precipitated one out of whatever one's out-of-body state was, back into the tank. If there was any danger under the LSD, the body's "emergency function" programs, the socalled survival programs, would be activated and I would be returned intact to the tank from wherever I was. This established a basic confidence in my own ability to survive and carry out the rest of the experiments.

Thus I was able to set up the basic belief, have confidence in the body to carry on its functions; leave it parked and go to other spaces; in case of an emergency you will be returned to your body.

After this initial set of experiments I lost my fear of doing the far-out series of experiments.

In the previous set of experiments without LSD in the tank, I had discovered that although not seeing my body I did not lose the reality of my body. Modes of detection of my body were present, other than just sight and hearing. This, too, is of use with the LSD in the tank. In that first twelve-hour experiment I went into the tank and came out of the tank five or six times during the twelve hours, reasserting my total perception of my body and increasing my conscious awareness of the vital processes.

Long before, I had established what I call the automatic bladder effect. Since the water is flowing through the tank, there is no problem with urine. One just goes ahead and urinates. In the earlier experiments in 1954-1958, I had found that if one just totally relaxes on the problem of urination, the bladder automatically empties about once every fifteen minutes. The first urination one experiences under these conditions is delightful. There is a sense of total enjoyment of the urine flowing after this initial response to the release of the civilized inhibitions. Finally, one doesn't even notice one's bladder is emptying. Since at the same time I was doing these experiments, I was on a very high protein diet, there was no problem with feces. I had purposely eliminated all carbohydrates and starch from my diet to cut down on the production of feces and gas. Previous experiments done at Cal Tech when I was a student and during my medical school days showed me that a high protein diet adds a lot of energy to the body, biological energy that is available for use in the province of the mind in the tank.

During that first experience with the LSD in the tank, I quickly found that it was very easy to leave the body and go into new spaces. It was much easier than in the first two trips with the guide. The lack of distracting stimuli allowed me to program any sort of a trip that I could conceive of. This freedom from the external reality was taken as a very positive point, not a negative one. One could go anywhere that one could imagine one could go. If one had the belief that one would be taken over by other beings, other entities, by states in which one would lose control, this happened. Therefore in the first trips I had to deal with my fear of "losing control."

I quickly discovered that a little bit of anxiety is a good thing. If the fear built up in these strange and wonderful spaces to a certain level, I automatically came back to my body. The reentry problem was solved by knowing or by having a basic belief that when too fearful I could and would return to my body (cf. R. A. Monroe's account, bibliography).

Thus I derived two basic postulates for taking further trips. The first postulate is that the body can take care of itself when one leaves it. The second postulate is that one can return to one's body if things get too tough out there. Later I was to find that as my tolerance for fear increased, I could stay longer in these spaces. I also learned that I didn't have to return to my body under an intense fear situation but could barge on through and move into another space without the necessity of coming back to the body space. As my navigation and piloting skills improved, and as my training of myself improved, I was thus able to move using fear energy converted into other energy modes. Finally, I was able to eliminate fear as a necessity and I was able to move through spaces without it. New motivations took the place of the old phobic ones. Energy conversion from negative to positive became realizable.

In the first tank experiment with LSD, the first space I moved into was completely black, completely silent, empty space without a body. The blackness stretched out to infinity in all directions. The silence extended out to infinity in all directions, and I remained centered at a single point of consciousness and of feeling. There was literally nothing in the universe but my center, myself, and the blackness and the deep silence. In a shorthand way, I called this "the absolute zero point." This became a reference point to which I could return in case things got too chaotic or too stimulating in other spaces. This was the central core of me, my essence in a universe with no stars, no galaxies, no entities, no people, no other intelligences. This was my safe place.

It is very hard to say how long in earthside time I stayed in this place on this first trip. I stayed long enough to become acquainted with it and to use it as a reference place to which I could return. It was the zero point of a vast coordinate system, leading in "n" different dimensions*, in n different directions away from this point. This point seemed to be the result of my scientific training. I had to have a reference zero from which I would move out onto various dimensions; a zero to which I could come back.

I wish to emphasize that this zero point was not in the body, it was out in a universe of nothing except silence and blackness. It was defined as out of the body, out of the universe as we know it. As I was to learn later, the illusion of blackness and silence meant that I was still holding on to the usual cognition spaces of the body. I was still holding onto the idea of blackness, the idea of silence, the idea of a central point of identity and consciousness. Later this was found to be unnecessary, except during extreme states when I needed a rest. At those times I would return to the zero point.

This zero point is a useful place. It is not complete separation

---

* n in mathematics is an arbitrary number, usually large. "n" dimension implies more than the usual three dimensions of space.

from one's previous ideas, but it is separation from the body. It is a space that still represents the darkness and silence of the tank, but with the body nonexistent. One's self still exists.

During this first trip I also defined other kinds of belief with which I would experiment. I would try to go to universes other than our consensus universe, universes I didn't necessarily believe existed, but which I could imagine. At first this was a test of the hypothesis that what one believes to be true becomes true. Before the trip, I didn't believe in these universes or spaces, but I defined them as existing. During the LSD trip in the tank I then took on these beliefs as true. After the trip, I then disengaged and looked at what happened as a set of experiences, a set of consequences of the belief.

For example, I assumed that there were civilizations way beyond ours, that there were entities in our universe that we normally cannot detect, but are there and have realities way beyond ours.

Suddenly I was precipitated into such spaces. I maintained myself as a central point of consciousness, of feeling, of recording. I moved into universes containing beings much larger than myself, so that I was a mote in their sunbeam, a small ant in their universe, a single thought in a huge mind, or a small program in a cosmic computer. The first time I entered these spaces, I was swept, pushed, carried, whirled, and in general beat around by processes which I could not understand, processes of immense energy, of fantastic light, and of terrifying power. My very being itself was threatened as I was pushed through these vast spaces by these vast entities. Waves of the equivalent of light, of sound, of motion, waves of intense emotion, were carried in dimensions beyond my understanding. The first time this happened, I became extremely anxious and jumped back into my body.

I then became intensely exhilarated and went into a high while in my body. I got out of the tank and went out into the sunlight, looking up into the sky, savoring the fact that I was a human on a planet. For the first time since childhood, life was precious; the sun, the sea, the air, all were precious. My body was precious. My feelings of energy and of extreme exhilaration continued. I sat and contemplated the wonder of our creation, of the creation of our planet. An hour or so later, I climbed back into the tank and launched into other regions. I had had enough of the vast spaces, the vast entities for a while. Now I attempted to contact other systems of life, more on a level with our own, and yet alien to us. I moved into a region of strange life forms, neither above nor below the human level, but strange beings, of strange shapes, metabolism, thought forms, and so forth. These beings reminded me of some of the drawings I had seen of Tibetan gods and goddesses, of ancient Greek portrayals of their gods and of some of the bug-eyed monsters of science fiction. Some of these forms were constructed of liquid, some were constructed of glowing gases, and some were solid state "organisms." The vast variety of possible life forms in the universe passed before me. In this particular space, they were not involved with me, I was not involved with them. I was an observer watching them. They were apparently unaware of me and were going about their particular businesses without interfering with me or paying any attention to me. I was an observing point in their universe, uninvolved and merely there picking up what I could of their way of life and recording it, somehow.

I came back to my body from that experience with full respect for the possible varieties of life forms that can exist in this universe. I was awestruck by the varieties of creation, by the varieties of intelligences that exist in our universe.

My next trip was down into my own body looking at various systems of organs, cellular assemblages, and structure. I traveled among cells, watched their functioning and realized that within myself was a grand assemblage of living organisms, all of which added up to me. I traveled through my brain, watching the neurons and their activities. I traveled through my heart, watching the pulsations of the muscle cells. I traveled through the blood, watching the business of the white blood corpuscles. I traveled down through my gut tract, getting acquainted with the bacteria and the mucosal cells in the walls. I went into my testes and became acquainted with the formation of the sperm cells. I then quickly moved into smaller and smaller dimensions, down to the quantum levels and watched the play of atoms in their own vast universes, their wide empty spaces, with the fantastic forces involved in each of the distant nuclei with their orbital clouds of force field electrons and the primary particles coming to this system from outer spaces. It was really frightening to see tunneling effects and the other phenomena of the quantal level taking place. I came back from that trip realizing what a lot of empty space I had in myself and what vast energies were locked in the matter of my own body. Having seen nuclei disintegrate before my eyes, releasing fantastic radiation energies on a microscopic scale, I had a new respect for what I was carrying around and what I, in a sense, was at these levels of reasoning and functioning.

I then left the tank again and went into the bathroom. My belly felt full and distended as if I were pregnant. I became my own mother, pregnant, carrying me, myself, in my own belly. I suddenly realized that I was about to give birth to myself. I sat on the toilet and had a huge bowel movement, which was myself. Suddenly the humor of this peculiar division of myself giving birth to myself struck me. I had an ecstatic experience of total sexuality, of being a man and a woman, totally fused, giving birth as the "baby" dropped into the toilet. I realized that it was not me, not a baby, and yet at the same time, I lived through giving birth to myself as if I were my mother. I experienced my birth as she had experienced it, as a totally exhilarating event, giving rise to a new living entity. I went back into the tank and went off into other spaces, far from this planet.

Later, I was to notice that there was a definite rhythm to leaving the body, to coming back and finding out something new about the body from a new perspective in the far-out spaces. This back and forth between the far-out and the very close-in was a rhythm I seem to have come across almost as a natural discovery. This seemed to be my tendency, to move as far out as possible and then to move in as close as possible. I gradually learned that the goal was to do neither of these but to stay in as close as possible and be as far out as possible, simultaneously.

Over the years I have gradually gone from an "either/or" to a "both" in regard to these spaces. I am far-out and close-in simultaneously. After the first few experiments in the tank, things began to shape up in far better fashion. My role as an explorer became much clearer. I was cleaning up a lot of the materials that were hindering me. I discovered that I had to clean up my hindrances to imagining or metaprogramming anything and everything. All and everything that one can imagine exists. Literally one is tuned in to the cosmos with all of its infinite variations. Once I had arrived at this basic belief, the possibility of tuning in on any one of the infinite varieties in the universe, I went on a high, became extremely exhilarated and launched further into the explorations.

Before my second tank trip, I suddenly was thrown a fantastic hindrance. I had a migraine attack, the first one in nine months since my first two LSD trips. Allow me to review what a migraine attack meant to me. I had an excruciating pain in the right side of my head which lasted eight hours. I had been having these attacks about once every 18 days for the past 40 years. My thinking was very much simplified during these attacks, to the point where I was an oversimplified human being. During the period in which the migraine pain was me, I could not think effectively and broadly. I could not function and had to lie down in a darkened room. This was the original negative stimulus for taking LSD. I wanted to get rid of my migraine, to solve it, never to have another attack. I temporarily abandoned the tank and tried a trip lying down on the bed, to examine my migraine. The facts I had learned in three years of training analysis about my migraine paraded before me in a very graphic form. First a space appeared in which the neurological lesion theory of migraine attacks was epitomized.

There is a very large red neuron, which is the cause of the migraine. It is a pain neuron that can start firing and maintain its firing for eight hours. There are yellow dendritic endings on this neuron, yellow axons going off to the cortex from this location in the mesencephalon. These are excitatory yellow neurons. There is another set of dendrites ending on this neuron, which are blue. These are the control endings that prevent the red neuron from firing. These two, yellow and blue, go into the cerebral cortex. However, each of these sets has connections into other ports of the brain not under the control of cortex, into the hippocampal region and into the archeo-cortex, where basic animal survival programs are stored. These can activate the migraine when I am overexcited.

I lay there and traced out all of the circuits, all of the programs that I conceived could cause the migraine and other programs that could terminate an attack. I spent some time in going through this theoretical structure for the explanation of migraine. I then put that aside and went into another space, having to do with the migraine. At this time, the side of my head where the pain occurred developed a "hole."

This hole was on an interface between our universe and another one that contained alien demonic forms who were pouring into my head from their universe. I shrieked in terror as they approached and entered my head. During the LSD trip, I had a horribly real migraine attack while I was under attack from these demons. I went into a terror panic space, suddenly realized where I was, came out and terminated the whole experience by closing off the hole from that universe.

I then went through a long sequence in which God ("out there") had given me migraine as a warning against overdoing things, as a warning of excess beyond wisdom, as a punishment for committing sin.

All of this then became hooked up to my sexuality and I went through long sequences having to do with punishment for not attaining spiritual enlightenment and for having gone into the animal world of sexual intercourse. This quickly reminded me of the initial LSD trip in which I had projected the goddess and the female gorilla onto the body of my guide. I was then able to see the irrationality of these past programs. I realized that they were still active, that I would not be able to erase them, but that I could allow for their existence. The right side of my head became filled with joy, exhilaration, and new feeling.

Temporarily freed of this old hindrance, I was then able to go back to the tank experiments. Armed with my new knowledge of how to pilot and navigate in these difficult spaces, I then launched a series of eight experiments having to do with suprahuman, supraself kinds of spaces.

One of my major aims here was to get back to the place with the two guides that I had been in during the coma in the hospital when I was close to death. I had been forced into an extremely anxiety-fear-filled space with lots of pain in my head. The aim this time was to see if I could get into this same space without this threat of death hanging over me. Each of the previous times when I had met the two guides, I had been in a state of fear, fear of the loss of life. Somehow the knowledge that the guides had given me in this last foray into their region armed me with a loss of the fear of death. Their assurance that I could come back to their region at any time that I needed to, and their assurance that my time had not yet arrived for my leaving my body permanently gave me the strength and the courage to try this experiment.

All of the previous experiments had been done with one hundred micrograms of pure lysergic acid diethylamide tartrate (Sandoz). For this experiment I decided to use a higher dose. I started with 100 micrograms, waited an hour and took another 100 and then in another hour took another 100 for a total dose of 300 micrograms. I based the increased dosage on the literature. The three hundred micrograms had been used to induce deep religious experiences in alcoholics. I chose the divided dose schedule rather than one dose so that I could maintain my piloting and navigation skills and storage capacity. I wanted to be able to control my movement out of the body. During the first hour I worked on the prime directive program of relaxing the body, letting it take over its vital functions. After the second dose, I went to the zero point of infinite darkness and infinite silence. By the end of the third hour with the third dose, I was ready to try to get into the space of the two guides.

Previously, I had tried to figure out how to get into that space without the fear and the pain. Somehow or other they had transmitted to me that I could return any time that I wanted to return. Therefore, all I had to do was to relax completely and "define" this space to be the space where I was going. Having been there previously, it turned out that this was the proper procedure. I defined myself in their space and suddenly I was there in their space.

I became a bright, luminous point of consciousness, radiating light, warmth, and knowledge. I moved into a space of astonishing brightness, a space filled with golden light, with warmth, and with knowledge.

I sat in the space without a body but with all of myself there, centered. I felt fantastically exhilarated with a great sense of awe and wonder and reverence. The energy surrounding me was of an incalculably high intensity, but I found that I could stand it this time. I could feel, see, and know out in the great vastness of empty space filled with light. Slowly but surely, the two guides began to come toward me from a vast distance. At first I was barely able to detect them in the background of high intensity light. This time, they approached very slowly. As they approached their presences became more and more powerful, and I noticed that more and more of them was coming into me. Their thinking, their feeling, their knowledge was pouring into me. As they approached, I could share their thinking, their knowledge, and their feeling at an incredibly high rate of speed. This time they were able to approach closer before I began to get the feelings of being overwhelmed by their presence. They stopped just as it was becoming almost intolerable to have them any closer. As they stopped, they communicated, in effect, "We will not approach any closer as this seems to be your limit for closeness with us at this time. You have progressed since we were together last. As we told you, you can come back any time once you learn the routes. We are sent to instruct you.

"You now have x number of years left to inhabit the body that you are given. If you wish to stay here now, you may. However, the discovery of your body in the laboratory tank in the Virgin Islands will leave a mess back there for others to clean up. If you go back to your body, it will mean a struggle and large amounts of work in order to get through the hindrances you carry with you. You still have some evasions to explore before you can progress to the level at which you are existing at the moment. You can come and permanently be in this state. However, it is advisable that you achieve this through your own efforts while still in the body so that you can exist both here and in the body simultaneously. Your trips out here are evasions of your trip on your planet when looked at in one way. When looked at in another way, you are learning and your ability to come here shows that you have progressed far along this path. Now that you have made it without pain and without fear, you have made progress.

"Your next assignment, if you wish it, is to achieve this through your own efforts plus the help of others. So far you have been doing your experiments alone, in solitude, and have learned some of the ways here. Your next assignment is to contact others like yourself who have these capacities, help them, and learn from them how to carry out this kind of existence. There are several others on your planet capable of teaching you and also of learning from you. There are levels beyond where you are now, and where we exist, to which you can go with the proper work.

"Thus, as part of your assignment, you are to perfect your means, while staying in the body, of communicating with this region, with this space, with us. There are other methods than LSD plus solitude for achieving these results. There are other means than fright and pain." They gave me a very large amount of additional information, but on this information they placed a seal. They said that I would forget it when I came back into the body until such time as this information was needed. Then, it would be there and I would use it, "remembering" what they had put into me.

I came back from this trip totally exhilarated, feeling extremely confident and knowing exactly what I had to do, but there was a quality of sadness about the return, a bit of grief that I was not yet ready to stay in that region. I spent five days working through what they had told me. I found that the future plan for my life was unfolding quite automatically. I was to finish the work with the dolphins and get onto work with humans. I was to get through some more of my hindrances and find out more about my evasions to getting on with the mission.

I then went on to do other experiments with the LSD in the tank, penetrating through many of my hindrances and discovering more of my evasions. During these experiments I felt some sort of unseen guidance as to what to do next. I began to feel the presence of the guides without going to their spaces. In each new universe that I penetrated, I felt their presence protecting me from the huge entities that inhabit these other spaces. In the last of this series of experiments, I was shown the whole universe as we know it.

I am out beyond our galaxy, beyond galaxies as we know them. Time is apparently speeded up 100 billion times. The whole universe collapses into a point. There is a tremendous explosion and out of the point on one side comes positive matter and positive energies, streaking into the cosmos at fantastic velocities. Out of the opposite side of the point comes antimatter, streaking off into the opposite direction. The universe expands to its maximum extent, recollapses, and expands three times. During each expansion the guides say, "Man appears here and disappears there." All I can see is a thin slice for man. I ask, "Where does man go when he disappear, until he is ready to reappear again?" They say, "That is us."

During this experience I was filled with awe, reverence, and a fantastic feeling of smallness, of not amounting to very much. Everything was happening on such a vast scale that I was merely an observer of microscopic size, and yet I was more than this. I was part of some vast network of similar beings all connected, somehow or other responsible for what was going on. I was given an individuality for temporary purposes only. I would be reabsorbed into the network when the time came.

After this experiment, word came that LSD was no longer to be used and each of the investigators was to send his supply back to Sandoz. New laws came into effect, making it illegal to use LSD any more, except under strictly limited conditions. Now I could understand why people were frightened of LSD; now I could understand why it seemed necessary to stop the legal use of LSD.

My interpretations of the above experiences varied depending on my real situation on this planet. There were times when I denied these experiences, denied them any validity other than my own imagination. There were other times when I felt that they had a very secure reality and I had a feeling of certitude about their validity. The two guides warned me that I would go through such phases of skepticism, of doubt. One thing that does stick with me is the feeling of reality that was there during the experiences. I knew that this was the truth. At other times I have not been so sure. Apparently I am in a position of waiting and seeing. Meanwhile I have tried other approaches to get into these same spaces, not using LSD in the tank, but other methods, such as hypnosis and group efforts. These are discussed in another part of the book.

Chapter 4
FOLLOWING INSTRUCTIONS AND GOING WITH THE FLOW

At the close of the 1964-1965 series of experiments, and with the new laws in regard to LSD, it became very difficult to continue LSD research in the United States, but of the original 210 investigators there were only six left who were willing and authorized to continue the work. In the new atmosphere of suspicion, distrust, and fear, I decided not to continue the work until the atmosphere cleared. I took this intervening time to follow the instructions of the guides and to clean up the messy details of my life.

In their communications with me the guides had made it very clear that there were many unsatisfactory aspects to my life, i.e., that I had accumulated a great deal of responsibility in the form of professional colleagues, employees, family, children. Before I could progress forward and move deeper and in a more thorough fashion into these far-out spaces it would be necessary for me to solve the problems of my planetside obligations.

The planetside obligations consisted mainly in the rather large dolphin project that I was directing. My activities consisted in doing and encouraging others to do research on the brains and communication of the bottlenosed dolphin. The Karma that I had accumulated with respect to dolphins was a very peculiar one.

Quite early in the dolphin research, around 1955, I had realized that the dolphins have a very large brain, larger than ours, and that they were far more developed than we in strange and alien ways. From 1959 until 1966 I had been working on the problem of communicating with these beings. To do this, I was using the classical methods of catching dolphins and putting them into confinement in a laboratory. The work was being done by two groups, one in St. Thomas and the other in Miami, Florida. In Miami the group was mainly the brain research group. In St. Thomas it was mainly the communication group.

During the LSD experiences in the tank in the Virgin Islands, from 1964 to 1966, I had come upon the powerful set of concepts of "going with the flow," of following instructions of the guides, and of feeling the pulse of the universe here on the planet earth. Partly this comes from inside one's self and partly from other sources, at present unknown. The instructions of the guides epitomized the sources unknown.

In the awe, reverence, and wonder of exploring the many spaces present inside myself and in the universe, I found that I was developing a very powerful ethic. This ethic was beginning to regulate my life, my attitude, my relations with others, and my professional career. This ethic I epitomized in *The Mind of the Dolphin** when I said that I had borrowed Erik Erikson's rephrasing of the Golden Rule, "Do unto others and not do unto others what

---

* Doubleday, Garden City, N.Y., 1907.

you would have the others do unto you and not do unto you. The others are to include other species, other entities, other beings in this universe."

I finished the book, *The Mind of the Dolphin*, in 1966; it was published in 1967. At the time of publication I had all of the information that was needed to carry out the instructions of the two guides and to follow this new ethic. However, to do so was going to cost me a lot of inconvenience, a lot of friends, a lot of pain, and my family.

I suddenly realized that I must stop the dolphin research. It was not being done in consonance with the new ethic. What I was doing and allowing to be done in my name was counter to where I wanted to go and hence it must be eliminated.

If I was to realize my desire to move into these regions, these new spaces, and communicate with these new entities, the dolphin project would have to be finished and thoroughly done over. The only way that I could see to do this effectively was to completely eliminate the whole then-current dolphin project and wait for a number of years until a proper one could be designed and carried out. As I wrote in *The Mind of the Dolphin*, the new project would mean complete freedom on the part of the dolphins to come and go as they pleased, rather than as we pleased. In that book it was proposed that a house be built by the sea. Part of the house would be flooded so that the dolphins could enter and be a part of the family life in that house. Both Margaret Howe (my associate) and I came to this conclusion after the dedicated communication efforts Margaret made in the dolphin laboratory in the flooded rooms in St. Thomas.

To clear the way for the new project, based on entirely new assumptions, the current projects were to be closed down.

The day that this clear decision came to me, and before I'd had a chance to communicate it to my colleagues, one of the dolphins in the Miami laboratory stopped eating. During the subsequent three weeks, despite powerful medical aids to recapture her appetite, she wasted away. During the next three weeks, four more dolphins committed suicide by refusing to eat or breathe. Before the remaining three could commit suicide, I decided to let them go at sea.

They were released in a tidal boat basin connected by a narrow channel to the sea. The oldest of the three we guessed to be about forty years old; the other two were very young – three to five years old. Before the old one would allow the two younger ones to go to sea, he cruised them around the boat basin and kept them down in the water. They kept trying to jump up to look into the boats and to respond to humans waving at them. He knew that this would lead to their deaths at sea. Large numbers of people carry guns in their boats and shoot at dolphins that insist on showing themselves. This task took the older dolphin about three hours. When he finally achieved his aim of keeping them down, they all left through the channel to the sea, and that was the last we saw of them.

We hid ourselves behind a wall so that they did not see us or they would have come back and stayed around. We had decided to make it a clean break, and so hid ourselves in order to watch what happened.

The original projects in our laboratory had been set up on the basic premise that, until we demonstrated scientifically the excellent quality and size of the dolphin brain in detail to the scientific community, we had no basis for others joining us in our belief that they are highly developed beings. They are comparable, if not superior to humans, in strange and alien ways. I had agreed with the neuroanatomists to sacrifice three dolphins at the beginning of the project so that they would have sufficient anatomical material of first-class quality for this brain anatomy demonstration. Even at the time I had doubts about the ethical correctness of allowing this kind of work to be done. However, I approved of it in the sense of generating scientific data, and hence propaganda, for the dolphins to be accepted as first-class biological organisms. I thought that this kind of acceptance by the scientific community was necessary in the future for our best relations with the dolphins. However, I still feel uneasy about this kind of justification.

At the peak of the dolphin research we had thirty people working on this research. My ethical duty here was to close down the research in such a way that these people would not be left without jobs. During the subsequent year, places were found for these people. The dolphin brain group was moved intact to another scientific laboratory at Worcester, Massachusetts. Our computer was sent back to the National Institute of Mental Health at Bethesda, Maryland. The accumulation of scientific apparatus was split between the brain research group in their new location and the Maryland Psychiatric Research Center to which I was moving to continue LSD work under legal auspices.

During the 1964-1966 series of experiments with LSD, the relationship between my wife and myself had become intolerably strained. In the subsequent retirement of all of the dolphin projects, she and I became separated. The accumulated strains between us became so painful that it was necessary to terminate the relationship.

In the summer of 1968, the last of the dolphin papers, entitled "Reprogramming the Sonic Output of the Bottlenosed Dolphin," was published in the *Journal of the Acoustical Society of America* in the July issue. This paper summarized my position in regard to the present state of the art of communication with the bottlenosed dolphin. It added considerable technical detail to what I had written in *The Mind of the Dolphin*, published the previous year. The new ideas derived from the LSD tank experiments, *Programming and Metaprogramming in the Human Biocomputer* view of the brain was applied here to the dolphins. Instead of using the limited psychological framework of conditioned reflexes, negative and positive reinforcement, and stimulus-response, I derived a new set of theories and procedures based on the theory called "reprogramming."

This particular theory we deal with in greater length in this book. The basic postulate is that the dolphin has a very large biocomputer, which can be reprogrammed through his natural inputs and outputs in a continuous interlocking feedback relationship with the human and his biocomputer and his natural inputs and outputs, aided by instrumental means.

During the transition period, while I was transferring the dolphin work to others, I pursued a peculiar effect we had noticed when working with the communication systems of the dolphin. In order to study the dolphin humanoid vocalizations, we put what the dolphin said onto a repeating tape loop where we could study it. We then had a group of people guess what the dolphin had been saying. We obtained a list of, say, ten different words that they thought the dolphin was saying. To complete our study, we then had to take the vocalization of the human, which had just preceded the dolphin vocalization, and put that on a tape loop. We quickly found that listening to a repeating word in clear high-fidelity English generated more alternates than did the dolphin emission. If one listens to a tape loop of a repeated word for fifteen minutes, one may hear as many as thirty different words other than the one which is on the tape loop. We did an extensive study of the word "cogitate." We exposed something of the order of three hundred subjects to this word for periods of fifteen minutes to six hours. We asked each subject to write down the words that he heard or to report them with a microphone on another channel of the same tape recorder.

From these three hundred subjects we got on the order of 2,300 different words. Three hundred of these words were in the dictionary; the rest were words that we do not ordinarily use, i.e., nondictionary words as we began to call them. In this work I received the very enthusiastic contributions of Margaret Naesser, a student of linguistics from the University of Wisconsin. Margaret had tremendous energy and initiative and carried out the study using the IBM 360 computer system at the University of Illinois to analyze our results. Dr. Heinz Von Foerster at the biocomputer laboratory was intrigued by our results and arranged for us to use the computer.

The computer analyses showed that, for each sound slot in the word "cogitate," the human biocomputer on repetition turns over and selects other sounds which one then hears as if coming from the stimulus word outside. Each such sound is called a phon. We found that on the average people tended to make twelve phon slots in the original stimulus word "cogitate," The minimum number of slots was 3 and the maximum number was 26. The number of substitutions of sounds in each of the twelve slots was different. For the first slot, there were 13 substitutions. In the second, 44 different sounds could be brought in, and so on.

It turned out that this repeating word effect made it possible to demonstrate very rapidly to live audiences their own biocomputer operations. This is the reason that I went on with this work and made the transition from the dolphin to the human through the repeating word effect. It was an extremely convenient way of demonstrating to people their own self metaprogramming and the various concepts of the biocomputer.

In addition to hearing alternate words when being exposed to the repeating word stimulus, I found that certain people went through various kinds of trips. In one audience of two hundred people, we found that something like 10 to 12 percent of the people tripped out and did not report anything about the alternates that they heard. When I was able to quiz two of these people about what had happened, they described trips very much like the ones I had found in the isolation tank. In addition, we found that we could program the alternates a person would hear by various means.

To see the programmability of the alternates that were heard, the subject would listen to the repeating word for an hour and write down all of the alternates he heard and print them on cards.

Next, the subject would turn on the repeating word and listen to it while looking at the cards one at a time. He relaxed, and then, as he turned up a new card, he heard the alternate printed on that card. This experiment showed that visual input can program what is heard. We also found that peripheral vision, that is, the vision which is off the main axis from where one is looking, could also program what was heard. We printed alternates with very large letters on cards and brought them into the peripheral vision of the subject while he was listening to the repeating word. He then reported out loud what he heard. The word that was being brought in from the periphery, in spite of the fact that he could not read it consciously, started programming what he heard. This was a "programming" gradient from the farthest reaches of peripheral vision at 90 degrees to the optic axis in toward the focal center on the optic axis. Just before the subject could read the word consciously, that is, where it was still far enough off the central axis so that he could not read it consciously, the word was programming 90 percent of what he heard. This experiment demonstrated that people are constantly being programmed below levels of their awareness by the periphery of their vision. It is probably a good thing that this is true. It allows us to drive a car and to walk and to do various other tasks, including reading in a smooth fashion, without having to think about everything that happens.

The human biocomputer is constantly being programmed, continually, simply and naturally, below its levels of awareness, by the surrounding environment.

We noticed that some subjects were quite upset with these effects, which were beyond their immediate conscious control. They would not accept the fact that their brain was reading a word and registering the meaning of that word below their levels of awareness. No matter how hard they tried, they could not read the word unless they put their visual axis directly on the word, thus spoiling the experiment. To avoid such effects, of course, we had an observer looking at their eyes and any cases in which they let their eyes move were discounted. This kind of upset was easily corrected by continuing the demonstrations. As the person got used to such results and accepted them, he no longer became upset by the unconscious operations of his biocomputer. Later, I was to use this effect to show people some of the projection mechanisms in their own biocomputer in workshops at Esalen Institute.

From the repeating word effect, I learned something about going with the flow, relaxing and allowing instructions from some place else to run my biocomputer. If one relaxes totally while listening to the repeating word, one can quickly find all of the phenomena that I have described above. However, if one is "up tight" and refuses to really "let go" even though one would like to let go, these phenomena just do not occur as frequently.

My further lessons in going with the flow and following instruction were given at Topeka, Kansas, by Dr. Ken Godfrey and his colleague, Helen Bonny.

I started a series of experiments with Ken and Helen on hypnosis. I wanted to find out if I could achieve the same states with hypnosis as I achieved in the 1964-1966 experimental series with LSD. I also ran into some very powerful mental telepathy experiences under these circumstances, which were a further demonstration that if one went into the flow and followed the instructions of the two guides, various things would happen that are not explicable by consensus science means.

In Topeka, the three of us, Ken, Helen and myself, first became very deeply acquainted with one another in a six-hour session, in which we barred no holds in regard to what we were and what we wanted to do. This kind of a preliminary conference in depth is very important in order to be able to relax enough with one another to get the programming effects of the "hypnotic trance." In order to relax enough to enter these special "trance" states, one must be thoroughly acquainted with and trust the others.

At the first session, it was decided that I would try to go deep, and they would stay at lighter levels of trance. I would try to get back to the region of the two guides.

I knew I could get to that region under threat of death or with LSD in the tank – that is, isolation combined with a chemical. The point of this experiment was to see if I could get to this region by nondrug, nonisolation methods in the presence of other people.

Ken was the programmer and Helen gave me support as I went deeper. In the first experiment, I came upon various hindrances to getting to the guides. As I was going deep, trying to reach the region of clear golden light, the golden light appeared on the left but a very dark threatening cloud appeared on the right. I felt deep evil upon evil coming in from other dimensions on the right side. The right side is the only side on which my migraine attacks occur. Helen Bonny was on the right side; Ken on the left. The split in my being was good on the left and evil on the right. This split was finally abolished when Helen started working on the entities and forces coming from the right.

The experience here was very similar to the one in which I worked on my migraine with LSD. Then a "hole" in my head opened up into a universe and evil entities came into my head from the right. Helen and Ken accepted this evasion of going deeper and programmed me out of it.

Suddenly the evil blackness withdrew and the golden light took its place over my whole being and visual field. The two entities or guides did not appear but their presence was felt. I received various instructions from them about continuing on the path that I had chosen. I felt a very great approval of what we were doing, and a great satisfaction and a sort of blessed state came over me. I was in the flow and doing the correct thing following their previous instructions. This was a very rewarding experience.

That night I went back to my hotel room after the experiment. I had been thinking about my human guide of the first two LSD trips before I went to bed. In bed, I immediately went into deep trance.

I became a point center of consciousness, radiance, love, and warmth about two feet above the floor. I was in a bedroom, off the left-hand foot-end of a bed. I could see two table lamps, one on each side of the bed. There was no one in the bed. On the bed was a beautiful cover. I saw along the lefthand side of the bed. I was filled with feelings of love and warmth.

Suddenly, the cover over the bed on the left-hand side near the floor burst into flame. The flames traveled up and began to go over the top of the bed. I smelled smoke and moved back, feeling a sense of threat. I came back to the room in the hotel and suddenly realized that I had traveled out of my body from Topeka, Kansas, to Beverly Hills, California, and that I was in the bedroom of my first LSD guide.

I called her up on the telephone and just said, "What happened five minutes ago?" She said, "I was in bed with books all over the top of the bed reading. I got up to go to the bathroom, came back, couldn't find my glasses among all the books and grabbed the cover over the bed and violently pulled it off, throwing all of the books on the floor. I very briefly lost my temper. I found the glasses and climbed back into bed."

I then told her what I'd gone through. She agreed to report anything further that happened during the subsequent two days. She agreed that it was important that first she tell me what had happened to her rather than the other way around so that we would not be doing cross or parallel programming. In these experiments, I wanted to see if I was traveling and detecting what was going on in her particular regions. These experiments would have been improved if we had had a third observer to which each of us would have reported, but we decided that this was the way to do it at that time.

The next day Ken, Helen, and I repeated our experiment of the previous day. Once more a peculiar repetition from the past took place, and it appeared as if I was evading getting to the two guides.

As I went deep into trance this time, I suddenly was on another planet, not earth, in a deep cave, a very peculiar vertical cave with a spherical chamber at the bottom. Somehow, I did not know how to get out of this cave. I looked up through the vertical shaft and saw a blue light at the far end of the tunnel. I was threatened by the fact that at the edges of the shaft there were what I thought to be "solid state life forms," small cubical and rectangular creatures who were doing some sort of work that I couldn't understand around the edges of the shaft. They were very busy and covered the whole surface of the shaft. I estimated that none of them was larger than three to four inches across in the largest dimension.

Somehow I felt that I was trapped in this spherical chamber and that I did not dare go up the shaft for fear of what these creatures might do to me.

We had arranged that I would be able to report what was happening from the depths of trance and I reported what was going on to Helen and Ken. Helen then immediately said, "I will lift you up through the shaft without your touching the walls. Stay with me. Allow me to lift, and you will come up."

Immediately, I started rising through the shaft, came out through the opening in the surface of that planet, and saw the immense blue sky over my head and the very peculiar terrain of that planet.

It had a golden color to it. There was no green. There was nothing that I could describe in earthlike terms. It was of a very peculiar construction, very smooth, and quite unlike any earth scene that I have been in. There were some other beings on the surface of the planet, but at this point I was not interested in staying there, so I came back to the room in which the three of us were working.

Later that afternoon, Helen Bonny wanted to participate in the repeating word experiment. That afternoon we arranged to run her as a subject. We arranged the experiment in a soundproof room. While she was listening to the repeating word coming from a loudspeaker near the head of the couch on which she was lying, I was lying on another couch across the room and relaxing. As she would hear an alternate, she would repeat the alternate word out loud into a microphone. I noticed that as I became more and more relaxed, I was hearing alternates also, A peculiar effect emerged in that as she would say an alternate, I would hear another alternate, which was in answer to hers. The only importance of this observation is that it showed that I was very relaxed. I was allowing and going with the flow.

Suddenly the source of the repeating word, the sound, moved from the left-hand side of the room all the way across the room and came inside my head as if I was wearing earphones. My one part of me knew that the loudspeaker, out of which the repeating words were coming, was on the far side of the room but another part knew that it was inside my head.

I went with this effect, realizing then that I was in trance and that this was one of the reprogrammings of the perceptual field that can take place during this particular state of consciousness.

Suddenly, even though my eyes were closed, I was looking into a room filled with golden light. I saw a huge chandelier, an immensely beautiful chandelier, hanging from the ceiling. I was filled with warm loving feelings and a sense of childish delight and wonder at the beauty of this chandelier in this golden room. I felt the way I had in childhood at the prospect of seeing a palace, of being in a palace like those recounted in fairy stories. The chandelier had prismatic crystal pieces, hundreds of them hanging around the lights in the chandelier. The light being emitted was a soft golden glow.

After this experiment was over, I called up California and asked my former guide what had happened to her at 3 p.m. She said, "At five minutes to three, I looked at the clock and realized that I had to go pick up the children from school. I started down the stairs and looked at the chandelier hanging from the ceiling in the stairwell. I was overcome with a sense of its immense beauty and took a childish delight in admiring it and seeing its fabulous palacelike quality. I skipped on down the stairs watching it as I went, admiring it and thoroughly enjoying the experience."

I then told her what had happened at the same time to me at a distance of twelve hundred miles away. She was delighted and we agreed to meet for further exchange when I got back to California.

These two experiences in mental telepathy with my guide showed me one thing, and that is that somehow or other I got into the mind of the other person involved and shared her state. In both cases, her particular mood and emotion was transmitted to me as if I were her, the chandelier as a direct experience of my own and the burning bed cover as a symbolic transfer of her anger. In this latter case, it may be that I avoided experiencing the anger that she felt and created the symbolic representation myself.

In the third experiment with Helen and Ken, I went much deeper and approached the region of the two guides, but I was unable to really penetrate into the region. We then finished the series of experiments and I left for California.

I met with my guide (terrestrial type) and discussed the results of these experiments. She wanted to hear the tapes of the inductions in the hypnotic experiments. I put one on the tape recorder and we sat back to listen.

In this situation I knew what was going to happen next on the tape. I knew which one of us was going to speak, Helen, Ken, or I. My guide did not know. I again went into a light level of trance and apparently she did also, just listening to the induction procedure. The experiment in this particular case took about three minutes and the rest of the time Ken, Helen, and I were discussing the experiment and various other matters on the tape. Suddenly the guide said, "I think that I was there at that meeting of the three of you." I said, "Oh, how could you have been there, you were in California?" She said, "I know exactly what is going to be said next and who's going to speak." She proceeded to demonstrate this to me. As one person finished speaking she'd name the next one and what they were going to say. While she was doing this, I suddenly realized what was happening: she was inside my head listening to my memory of what had gone on. She did this for a period of about twenty minutes, recounting exactly the next thing coming up. Suddenly she broke it off and said, "I don't believe in mental telepathy at all! This can't be happening." I said, "Well, it is happening! You are definitely inside my head the way I was inside yours over the distance of twelve hundred miles." She finally accepted it and laughed with a childlike joy.

These experiments and experiences showed me that I really should investigate hypnosis more thoroughly. I decided to go to the laboratory of Ernest Hilgard at Stanford University, which was the only hypnosis research laboratory in a university that I knew of. I spent two weeks in Hilgard's laboratory reading the literature, getting acquainted with the field and being put through some experiments. First of all, they were interested in finding out how I responded to various of their tests. They put me through the "hypnosis susceptibility" test, which I later called the "hypnosis talent" test. My scores were very high, comparable to a group of high school students that they had recently run. They had found that, in general, as people became older, their talent for developing trance decreased. They were less willing to be programmed by an outside programmer.

If one is going with the flow and following instructions about conscious states, there is no real problem in allowing somebody outside to do that programming. However, if one fears outside programming and is afraid that that person is going to take advantage, or if one just fears outside programming in general, one cannot go into the deeper trance in this way. High school students were better than college students and college students were better than the older age groups at getting into trance states. Apparently, I was exceptional; I had been through LSD in isolation and I accepted outside programming much more easily. I was also more tolerant of going into these states. I could accept trance with a much greater degree of confidence than similar people in my age group.

I gave a seminar about the repeating word effect to a group in the hypnosis lab. I remember very well Professor Hilgard waiting a full eight minutes before he heard his first alternate. A smile broke out on his face as he heard his first alternate. He said later that he had not believed in the effect until that point, which was a good attitude to take. One should be skeptical of these things until one experiences them directly himself. However, I was very glad that he was willing to carry out the experiment and to hear his first alternate.

The speed at which people heard alternates seemed also to be a reflection as to how easily they were hypnotizable in other words, what sort of talent they had for relaxing and going with the flow. The youngsters all heard alternates immediately and went on and heard many, many more than the older people.

We found somewhat of a correlation between one's ability to go into trance and one's ability to hear alternates to the repeating word. I became acquainted with the graduate students in the department and heard many stories about their experiments with trance and the various effects that take place. Some of them were quite talented and could have out of body experiences and various other phenomena of the deep trance. In that laboratory, I learned many of the dimensions of personal experience that can be programmed into one's biocomputer. I learned that there are many, many different states and many, many different phenomena that one can experience, which are subsumed under the name trance phenomena.

I did not particularly like the terminology of hypnosis because it implied something special, something removed from one's ordinary experience and something available only to professionals. In my own experience, these states are natural, simple, easy, obvious – once one is willing to go with the flow. The human biocomputer is capable of many, many different states of consciousness and has a vast panorama of states that we do not normally allow to happen.

I learned that what I experienced under LSD in isolation and solitude in the tank was not really as far out as I thought it to be at the time. With relaxation techniques and concentration, one could probably achieve similar, if not identical, results.

While I was at Stanford, I heard about Esalen Institute and decided to go down to the Big Sur coast and see what Esalen was like. The particular weekend I decided to go, there was a symposium on "psychosis as a self-evolving experience." I went to listen to this symposium because, in my own thinking, psychosis was defined as something other than what it had been many years before. In my new way of thinking about states of consciousness, psychosis was just an unusual state of consciousness into which one had gone, and this somehow or other interfered with other people, and hence one was locked up.

I realized that the term "psychosis" was a cultural social term as well as a term having to do with internal states. As with many people, my realization grew when I read the books of two unconventional psychiatrists (Thomas Szasz's *The Myth of Mental Illness** and *Psychiatric Justice*,† and Ronald Laing's *The Politics of Experience*‡). The internal states present in psychosis can be multitudinous.

At this symposium, psychosis was discussed at length in these terms, and the various speakers ranged from a Polish and a Czechoslovakian psychiatrist to some of the Esalen staff people. Their conclusions were that psychosis, as looked at classically, has very little meaning. It is the states of consciousness and the confinement that lead to the evolution of self.

Several people present had been through psychotic episodes, and they reported how beneficial this was to their subsequent life. The thing of interest to me was that these people had been able to go into special states of consciousness and stay there for a day, weeks, or months. This seemed to me to be a surprising kind of talent. With LSD or the tank or both or with hypnosis, I had achieved these states only for a few hours. During these states, I was completely aware that if they were to persist beyond the time of the experiment, my close relatives, friends, and colleagues would be upset. The best thing to do was to come back instead of staying in these states. The essence of psychosis seems to be that one goes into one of these special states and then refuses to come back. One may even misuse the state to punish one's relatives or friends by forcing them to take

---

* New York Harper & Row, 1961. New York: Delta paperback, Dell, 1977.

† New York: Macmillan, 1965.

‡ New York: Pantheon, 1967. New York: paperback, Ballantine

care of one's physical self so that one can stay in that state.

Later I was to read the biography of Ramakrishna by Christopher Isherwood* and to appreciate that staying in these special states of consciousness in India was a good deal easier than it was here in the United States. In the case of Ramakrishna, he had a temple, a sponsor, and lots of helpers around so that he could stay in a state for hours, days, or weeks without anybody interfering with it. In fact, they would facilitate his state because he was known as a holy man. Thus I learned that the duration of a special state of consciousness is limited by the society in which it is taking place, by the social surroundings, by family, and by the arrangements that one can make for the outside world while one is in these states.

In the tank LSD experiments I had been lucky. They were done in a remote part of a remote island in the Caribbean with no possibility of interference. I had complete control of the surroundings and of the people who were in those surroundings so that there was no danger of their interfering with the states or of misusing the information of my being in those states. I stayed at Esalen for the three days of the seminar and became acquainted with the people and with the special environment that was set up there on the Big Sur coast. I learned something of the other people in Big Sur and of the advantages, for certain purposes, of living there.

After Esalen, I went to Maryland, where my new job was awaiting me at the Maryland Psychiatric Research Center at Spring Grove State Hospital.

---

* Ramakrishna and His Disciples. New York: Simon & Schuster, 1965. Hollywood, Calif.: Vedanta, 1965.

Several of my old friends and acquaintances were working there, and they had asked me to come and work with them in problems of research on LSD and isolation. I arrived in Maryland and found the research center was not yet finished. We had many conferences and did a lot of in-depth talking with one another, becoming thoroughly acquainted with one another in the fashion that Helen Bonny, Ken Godfrey, and I had done.

After several weeks, it turned out I was spending most of my time with Dr. Sandy Unger. We discussed at great length how to design and carry out experiments to find out some of the mechanisms of operation of LSD-25.

This group was one of the remaining six in the United States legally authorized by several government agencies to do research with LSD-25 within a certain limited context.

The group had been working for several years with LSD-25 in the treatment of alcoholism. They had selected the worst possible cases of alcoholism in the Baltimore area at the Spring Grove State Hospital and had treated them along the lines that Humphrey Osmond and Abram Hofer had found successful in Saskatchewan, Canada.

In brief, the method consisted of doing intensive individual psychotherapy with each patient an hour a day for three weeks. This led toward an intensive psychotherapeutic experience with LSD-25, followed up by continued psychotherapy for one or two weeks following the experience. The session itself was an energy-programming session with the psychotherapist doing the programming. There was also an intensive use of music during the session.

I had watched several of these sessions via motion pictures and television. I had read all the papers they had written on the subject and I had gone over their results very carefully with them.

In general, alcoholics with this degree of severity of alcoholism did not respond to any treatment. Each of these patients had been through multiple forms of therapy without having given up alcohol. It was quite impressive and exciting to see them give up alcohol for periods ranging from six months to five years with one single treatment of this sort.

The design of the experiment was such that authorization was given for only one LSD treatment per patient, and the results were to be evaluated over a long period of time. In order to evaluate scientifically whether or not the single-shot treatment worked, it was necessary to avoid giving a second treatment during the evaluation period of at least three to five years.

There was extensive psychological testing before the psychotherapy, and also after the LSD, during the follow-up period.

I decided that I could not know what was going on in this treatment until I had gone through such a session myself. I didn't feel that I could design effective research programs until I had experienced, as a subject, what the patients were experiencing. My justification for this is a long-standing scientific commitment that I'd made a lot earlier during my period of working in human physiology under H. C. Bazett at the University of Pennsylvania, while I was a medical student and in the years following. The rationale of human physiological and psychological investigations goes somewhat as follows:

If you are a scientific investigator interested in using human subjects, it is necessary that you follow J. B. S. Haldane's dictum: "You will not understand what is necessary in the way of scientific control unless you are the first subject in your experiments." Professor Bazett taught me this unequivocally.

When he wanted to find out what the end organs (the sensitive endings within the skin) were, he performed psychophysiological experiments with a cold bath alternating with a hot bath to determine the temperature sensitive endings in the foreskin on his penis. He marked these with ink, had himself circumcised and found through microscopic sectioning and staining techniques the end organs responsible for the sensations that he had recorded.

Later, when it was important for him to know the temperature within the human brain, he had thermocouples inserted in his own brain through his jugular vein from the neck region. He measured the temperature within the brain and blood flow through his own brain. He never asked anyone else to do what he had not already done on himself.

This was the scientific policy that I was following when I did the isolation tank work at the National Institute of Mental Health and in the Virgin Islands. I followed the same policy when I did the isolation work with the LSD. I did not ask any other subjects to do it until after I had done it myself. Sometimes, one does not use another subject after one has done it oneself, because one realizes either that it is not necessary on a second subject or that it is too dangerous to do on a second subject. One then waits for another mature scientific investigator to do it on himself. This point of view was used by Walter Reed in his experiments to find the cause of yellow fever. This has been a medical and scientific research tradition among the older mature investigators for many years.

In recent years there has been much talk and much regulation both within the National Institutes of Health themselves and in their grants to medical schools. They prohibit the use of human subjects until a jury of one's peers judges whether or not the experiments should be done. This was the restriction placed upon the psychotherapy experiments using LSD at the Spring Grove State Hospital. The protocol of the experiments was exposed to several committees for a decision as to whether or not the group that proposed the experiments would be authorized to do them. I went over the protocols of the proposal from the Spring Grove State Hospital. In no case was it proposed that investigators be exposed to the experimental procedure first.

This lack of involvement of the investigators in their own scientific research as first subjects comes from another line of tradition than the one that I have been brought up and trained in. The justification of the opposing school, if you wish, is as follows: the patient has a disease, say, cancer. The investigator does not have this disease, therefore, if you are trying some new therapeutic procedure to try to cure the disease, you can't use yourself because you don't have the disease to cure.

I do not agree with this argument at all. You should not do to a patient what you are not willing to do to yourself. You do not know whether or not you are willing to do it on yourself until you try it on yourself. Even if you don't have the disease, whatever the procedure is that you propose using, it should not be damaging enough to prevent you from doing it on yourself. If it is, it should not be done on others. Therefore, until you've proved to your own satisfaction that it is not damaging on animals, and then proved to your own satisfaction that it is not damaging on yourself, it is better not to use it.

Back in the fifties, this was the argument that I used against putting brain electrodes into humans. I knew from my animal studies that no matter how you put brain electrodes in a brain, some damage to the brain took place during the insertion procedure. Unless one was willing to undergo this amount of damage by inserting electrodes into one's own brain, I didn't feel that there was any justification for inserting electrodes into anybody else's brain. This turned out to be a very cogent argument in suppressing the use of brain electrodes.

I began to apply the same argument to the LSD work. I found that, in reality, at Spring Grove no one was doing psychotherapeutic work with LSD until they had been through the LSD session themselves as a training procedure. Therefore, when I arrived at Spring Grove, it was obvious that they were following the ethic that I was already following myself, despite the official protocol.

Even though I'd had extensive experience with LSD in the isolation tank under the particular conditions that I had set up for myself in the Virgin Islands, I had not taken LSD under the circumstances prevailing at Spring Grove. By that time, I had a very high respect for what LSD could do and for what it did do or what happens under the influence of LSD, which varies considerably with what is going on inside one's self and with what is going on in the surroundings at the same time. Therefore, until I had taken LSD, that is, in the "psychotherapeutic" setting used with the patients, I would not know what was really happening inside these patients. I would not know how that reflected on their getting rid of alcohol as a mainstay in their lives.

After several weeks of preparation, Sandy and I decided that it would be possible for me to have a session within the next few weeks. At the time, it was very hard to run sessions on the professional personnel because this was not authorized by all of the agencies concerned. The large national negative program on LSD was still highly operative, and the regulations were extremely restrictive. (Since then training sessions have been authorized.) We were proceeding on the high-level medical ethical tradition that the medical scientist does the first experiment on himself. We felt that eventually the committees involved, and the various agencies, would agree to this point of view. There really is no other way of getting the primary information that one needs. It was a scientific necessity to do "training sessions."

The reason for the restrictions on the use of LSD on professional personnel was the fear that LSD damaged the brain, and later the fear that it damaged the chromosomes. In the early sixties I proposed studying the problem of brain damage by giving experimental animals extensive amounts of LSD over a long period of time. As this project was about to start in 1966, the national fear built up to a point that made the project impossible to carry out. Those of us who had taken LSD a large number of times were extensively tested and found not to have damaged brains. However, this positive data could not be presented nor accepted in the hysterical atmosphere that had been generated by the national media against LSD.

There were also many rumors that scientific investigators had taken LSD and had either gone psychotic or had dropped out of their profession. I tracked down some of these rumors and found out what had happened to these various people. As far as I could make out, some of them had taken up rather untenable positions in regard to the use of LSD. The most famous case was Dr. Timothy Leary, who was not a medical scientist, but a psychologist without medical training. He was not acting in the scientific medical tradition in his presentations of a revision of our culture to incorporate LSD as some sort of a sacrament. However, there were enough such cases to cause various committees and administrators to realize that LSD could cause trouble in their own organizations. My attitude was that this was the first series of investigators to have taken the substance. In the initial high energy and rapid changes that they could evoke with it, they had misjudged the case and needed time to integrate what had happened.

During my own initial experiments, I had run across these same areas of hyperenthusiastic response to certain kinds of experiences in the tank. I had also learned that until one has spent a good deal of time thinking about these results afterward, it is wiser not to present the results in public. By the time that I did the experiments, we had several public examples of people who had gone the other path and had made this kind of mistake. Actually I should not say that they made a mistake. They taught us very valuable lessons. If they hadn't done what they did, we couldn't have done what we did. So, actually, we owe them a debt. Each of these persons showed us what the public reaction would be if we took a similar path, so we were able to avoid the pitfalls and proceed with the work until the law made it impossible.

In regard to brain damage, I felt that there was no damage, as did the others who had taken it. We were opposed by the idea that we didn't have insight into the damage of our own brains. We felt this was fear-filled nonsense, as did those who examined us for possible brain damage.

In regard to chromosome damage, we designed experiments to find out if there was any. These turned out to be completely negative. Even though the evaluation of the damage was done by a man who was quite set against the taking of LSD, he could not find any chromosome damage due to LSD per se. In regard to the possible damage to children conceived during an LSD trip, and to a pregnant mother taking LSD, we had lots of examples of people in the early days who were on psychotherapeutic regimens with LSD and who conceived and produced babies while taking LSD. I know of these children today, and they are really delightful people. There is no sign of damage whatsoever.

I am reminded of a cartoon that appeared in Cavalier magazine at that time during the height of the public controversy: A long-haired boy is looking up at a poster, and says, "They're grasping at straws." The poster is a picture of an adolescent with a big sign across it saying "LSD Causes Acne."

As the national negative program reached its height, the enthusiasm for proving LSD damaging captured the imagination of many scientists, and they set out to prove that it was damaging without really knowing what they were doing. Careful, subsequent testing proved these people to be overenthusiastic and quite wrong in their conclusions. If you wish to check these points, look at the papers published from Spring Grove State Hospital by the LSD research group.*

This, then, is the account of my transition period from the 1964-1966 series of experiments with LSD in the tank and the temporary withdrawal of my research interest in the dolphin communication study.

---

*Papers by Drs. Walter Pahnke, Stanislaf Grof, Charles Savage, and Albert Kurland from the Maryland Psychiatric Research Center, Catonsville, Md.

Chapter 5
A GUIDED TOUR OF HELL

In early January of 1969, I felt the pressure building up to go farther in my own quest, to continue explorations of the spiritual side of life and of the special spaces that I had been in during the 1964-1966 series of experiments.

In the midst of this pressure, I decided to go talk with Jean Houston and Bob Masters, a couple who had worked in the past with LSD, who had written a book on the subject, and who were working with hypnosis and altered states of consciousness. I respected their integrity, their interest, their love, and their competence to deal with these subjects. I called them up and drove 250 miles to their house.

During the next two days, we spent two eight-hour sessions going over the basic assumptions in their work and in mine. In the course of the conversation they mentioned that they had taken a suggestion of mine. During the hypnotic inductions for their more difficult cases, they evoked the aid of entities greater than the particular human subject.

This came from my experience with the two guides. I realized that most people will not accept programming from their peers. We do not like the people that we conceive of as our equals to program us. We know as much as they do, and we are a bit skeptical of the results. In the case of the two guides, I realized that I had appealed to entities (or even had created entities) greater than myself, and hence I could take their instructions.

Since I'd seen them last, Jean and Bob had tried this technique on their fifteen most difficult subjects. Most of these subjects had not been able to get into trance of any great depth. With the new program, all of them got into deep trance, received instructions, and reorganized their lives along the lines that they wanted.

I found this contact with Jean and Bob very invigorating, and on the trip back to my home in Maryland, I found the confirmation needed to go ahead and pursue my exploration.

Since the Topeka, Kansas experiences, Helen Bonny and her husband had moved to Baltimore. As soon as I got back to my house, I called up Helen and asked her if she could come and do a hypnosis experience that I needed in order to get on with my explorations. By coincidence she was free and able to come. Coincidences continued piling up. When events pile up in your favor one after the other in rapid sequence, I call this a *controlled series of coincidences*. The following account shows one such sequence.

With our usual induction technique Helen brought me into the region of the two guides. She went to the same place at the same time. No sooner did I arrive in this region than I was unequivocally told with a good deal of energy, "You have a job to do back down there on the planet. Go down and do it." I went back down into my body, tapped Helen on the shoulder, and told her the message. She came back and we worked on my basic conflicts with my mother in childhood. This had been a sticky area for some time. Some of it was not to be cleared up for another two years. Of course, at this time I didn't know this. Staying in the trance state, I went into a very deep feeling of being very close to mother. I felt that the earth was mother. At that point I got into a very deep grief space and cried for half an hour. Then the telephone rang.

It was Sandy. He asked, "Do you have a pair of headphones?" This was sort of a group code word for a training session since music is played during the session through headphones. I said, "No, but I have a very powerful pair of loud speakers."

This whole telephone call was a surprise to me. Sandy and I had not talked recently about doing the training session. We had not arranged any specific time, and it looked to me at that moment as an inspired coincidence that he should come to the same conclusion I did. The guides had just told me to get on back down to the planet and do the session. That was the work I was to do, the planetside trip work. I then told him about the session with Helen and jokingly he said, "When you cry, please stay in your body and don't do it in my house. There is water running down through the ceiling into the kitchen, so I have to shut the water off before I can come over. Your tears are too many gallons for my ceiling."

Helen then left, and within an hour Sandy arrived. We spent the next six hours doing the preprogramming for the training session. He probed and probed as to what I wanted to do during the session, where I wanted to go, what parts of my past life I wanted to get into, what I was dissatisfied with in the way I was running my life. We tried to discover where unconscious tape loops rather than conscious choices were dictating my actions. We did a very prolonged, deep, intensive consideration of my life.

The main problem centered around what we called my "stainless steel computer." This was operating without love in a coldly logical and rational way with no hope and with no involvement with a loved woman. It was a dehumanized way of operating. He then examined my fears of impotence and the fact that currently I did not know how to find a loved woman. I was on a frantic search for one, driven by some unconscious motivation. There was not enough joy in my life, not enough awareness of humor. These were the major points where I needed to get into some very deep regions.

On this particular training session, I was not to leave my body and go into far-out spaces, but I was to stay within the planetside trip and my dissatisfactions in that trip. I was not to use traveling in far-out places as an evasion of getting on with this examination.

In this preprogramming session, Sandy pushed me very hard, the way he pushed the alcoholic patients in the project. Anytime he felt me evading or steering around an unpleasant subject, he precipitated me right into the middle of it. He got behind my defenses and convinced me that it was important to get behind them very deeply.

The room in which we were to work was set up in such a way that I could lie down on the floor on a comfortable carpet between two very large loudspeakers. I made a selection of the records I wanted Sandy to play while I was under the influence of LSD and piled them carefully beside the phonograph. This room had been prepared in advance with carpets hanging on the walls to absorb the sound in order to avoid echoes and to cut out the external light, if any. There was a single floor lamp in the room for light. The environment was designed to be as nondistracting as possible.

In this session I was to learn some things that I had not learned in the 1964-1966 series of experiments in the Virgin Islands, though I was not to fully understand the implication of what took place in this session for approximately two years (1970).

We had arranged in advance to use a divided-dose technique: 100 micrograms and then an hour later 200 micrograms. The LSD was pure Sandoz.

During the initial hour with 100 micrograms we continued the work on the preprogramming, and after the 200 micrograms took over, I lay down on the floor between the loudspeakers to listen to the music. The music was at a very high volume.

Suddenly I was precipitated into what I later called the "cosmic computer." I was merely a very small program in somebody else's huge computer. There were tremendous energies in this computer. There were fantastic energy flows and information flows going through me. None of it made any sense. I was in total terror and panic.

I was being programmed by other senseless programs above me and above them others. I was programming smaller programs below me. The information that came in was meaningless. I was meaningless. This whole computer was the result of a senseless dance of certain kinds of atoms in a certain place in the universe, stimulated and pushed by organized but meaningless energies.

I traveled through the computer as a program that floated through other programs. I moved to its extreme outer limits. Everywhere I found entities like myself who were slave programs in this huge cosmic conspiracy, this cosmic dance of energy and matter which had absolutely no meaning, no love, no human value. The computer was absolutely dispassionate, objective, and terrifying. The layer of ultimate programmers on the outside of it were personifications of the devil himself and yet they too were merely programs. There was no hope or chance or choice of ever leaving this hell. I was in fantastic pain and terror, embedded in this computer for approximately three hours planetside time, but eternally in trip time.

Suddenly, a human hand reached into the computer and pulled me out. As I came out, I went from just a program in a senseless dance of atoms to a human body back in the room with Sandy. I found that Sandy, seeing my terror and panic, had grasped my hand in order to comfort me. In the fantastic release I cried and suddenly I was a baby again in father's arms and he was rocking me.

I went back inside. This time I watched as if I were outside the computer. I saw two programmers in human form who had a robot figure on a bench. The robot was me. One of them said, "If that repairman down there [meaning Sandy] can't get some love into this model, we will have to junk it." I came back, laughed, and told Sandy that all he was was a repairman of robots. I then went back inside myself. The two programmers were once again talking about the robot which was me. One of them said, "This one wants an erect penis." The other programmer picked an erect penis off the shelf and thrust it onto the robot. I came back laughing and all of my past loves flowed through me.

I felt mother flowing through my being, father flowing through my being and all of the women of my past life, one after another, flowing through me complete with love, warmth, and radiance. I was filled with love and melted with this vision of all of the past history of my own love.

I went back inside again and watched as a scintillating energy-filled computed maze appeared, filled with sparkly lights of different colors. Walking through the maze, sensuously undulating were many extremely attractive female humans. I knew that they were robots also. They had glittering gowns that hugged their voluptuous figures closely, showing their delicious hips and bosoms and narrow waists and extremely beautiful faces. I saw five or six of these slinking through the maze. I heard the voices of the two programmers discussing this scene and me. This time I was not in the scene but merely watching, witnessing.

One programmer said to the other, "If he does everything that we want him to do, we will reward him with the love of one of these women." I was horrified because I realized that these women were robots and not real humans. I came back and told Sandy I would accept all the programming of the two guides, but not Sandy's own.

I said this in a humorous and laughing fashion since I realized that our preprogramming was working. By this time I was beginning to come out of the LSD and to slow down to normal time. All of these episodes had taken place at a very high energy level, extremely speeded up. Here I can only recount the highlights and those things which occurred, which taught me something new.

I learned that certain basic assumptions were embedded in

my human biocomputer. These assumptions came from consensus sciences as I had learned it at Cal Tech and from reading.

Assumption No. 1 was that the origin of the universe, either from the big bang theory or from the new creation of matter in empty space theory, was purely a matter of chance. There was no God. There was no organizing intelligence like our own. There was only the happenstance of matter collecting in dust clouds, coalescing into stars and the stars being collected in huge numbers into galaxies. Our bodily origins were the result of certain kinds of molecules, certain kinds of atoms, being collected in a given place on a planet, the atmosphere of which was the result of a series of automatic processes. Certain temperatures, certain kinds of matter and energy, radiation, and a certain distance from the sun generated us from the primordial sea on the planet through a slow, very slow, process of evolution. Once living assemblages of matter took place, they gradually joined forces and finally generated the anthropoid series of organisms of which we were the end result. This, then, was the *cosmic computer* generating us.

There was no creation by God. There was no God. There was no creation for anything. Matter itself and energy itself happened to combine in the right way to generate living assemblages of matter. These were my basic beliefs that had to be challenged through the LSD session.

In order to get rid of these limiting beliefs, I had to construct them into a completely rational whole with all of the negative emotion connected with them. As I was to understand later, this was a major burning of my Karma. This episode was what the Sufis call "going to hell in order to realize heaven."

In my own estimation, the cosmic computer exposure was the most punishing experience I had ever had in my whole life. It was far more punishing than any nightmare that I'd had as a child. It was more punishing than any outside experience that I had ever had at the hands of any human being. The pain, the terror, the paranoid feelings were of the maximum energy that my organism could possibly have sustained without burning me out.

On subsequent analysis, it turned out that the two guides were present during the whole experience. The two guides were disguised as the two programmers. The work that they had told me to get down there and do was finally being tackled. My last bit of skepticism based on limiting scientific grounds was finally squeezed out of me. From this extremely low point, the only direction was up toward the positive, toward love, toward enlightenment. There was no other choice. I had traveled once again through the Valley of Death and come out whole.

During the next few days I was to experience and feel love of the intensity that I had felt earlier in my childhood. I was to go through grief, through all sorts of emotions that I had been blocking off and refusing to recognize because of my "scientific knowledge." For the first time, I began to consider that God really existed in me and that there is a guiding intelligence in the universe. The positive experiences that I'd had in the 1964-1966 tank experiments – with intelligences or entities higher than myself and with the two guides themselves – were a shared organized aspect of the universe, the Network.

During the subsequent month, I was to find how negative aspects of my science had kept me away from humanity. I was now precipitated very strongly into the planetside trip with the human species. I was to see that, in one way, I had used the dolphins to stay away from my own species. I began to see that I needed further help in grounding myself securely on the planetside trip and in learning more about my evasions of loving. This training session opened up a whole new region of experience for me. I became quieter, more contemplative, more meditative, and more considerate of my fellow human beings.

An opportunity came to travel to California for a scientific meeting. I took the opportunity to meet some of the people on the West Coast, some of the people who understood LSD and the LSD spaces. I traveled in the Berkeley-San Francisco area, the Menlo Park area, and finally ended up at Esalen Institute in Big Sur, California.

On my visit to California the previous summer, I had met Alan Watts and had spent four hours with him discussing the deeper aspects of the universe, the basic religions of the East, and the deeper meanings of life as a human being. I was delighted to find that he was giving a seminar that weekend at Esalen which I could attend. I was very impressed with Alan's command of the language and his flow of descriptions of the mystical way of life.

As I stayed on at Esalen I became more and more impressed with the environment, the people, the possibilities of my moving there. In San Francisco I'd spoken to Dick Price and to Mike Murphy, founders of Esalen, about the possibilities. They had arranged for me to give a workshop in March at Big Sur. During the first few weeks of February, I stayed on at Big Sur and, with the help of some of the staff, began investigating myself and the possibilities of further change in my way of life. I became acquainted with the late Fritz

Perls and the people around Fritz; Virginia Sutton was a great aide to me in seeing some of my tape loops (hang-ups) operating below levels of awareness.

She demonstrated unequivocally some of my projection processes, and especially those onto a woman. With her help, I went through some very painful areas, which resulted in my expanding my awareness into my own unconscious games with a woman. I set up a game in which I apparently loved a woman, but in reality what I was doing unconsciously was trying to separate her from another man.

This program apparently went back to my very early childhood when my younger brother was born, when I was two and a half years old. The child of the time had the concept that the younger brother was displacing him with his mother, which of course he was; this led to rage and the start of this particularly nasty game of constantly trying to win mother back at the expense of another male. With Virginia's help, I was also able to see that my life was going in the direction of the Esalen type of life rather than the Spring Grove research type of life. On the trip back to Spring Grove, I made up my mind to give it up. This led to a lot of disappointment in my colleagues at the Psychiatric Research Center. The decision was not entirely unexpected, however.

I arranged to leave the center all of the scientific apparatus that I had brought with me. (This later allowed one of the ex-graduate students from the two weeks I'd spent at Hilgard's Laboratory to set up a proper biofeedback and hypnosis laboratory.) I resigned as of March 7, 1969 and moved to Esalen to start my new life.

In a conference with Dick Price, he set up a six weeks' series of workshops for me to take. During that same period, I was to give one of my own.

My first weekend at Big Sur was in a workshop with Bill Schutz and fifty-nine other people. Many impressive things happened. I was amazed at how a quiet programmer like Bill could get people to do things that they had not dared to do before, and to do it very rapidly in order to realize a greater human freedom.

For example, we were all standing in a rather small room, a room called Maslow at Esalen. Sixty people were standing pretty close together. Bill gave a very quiet eight-minute talk, at the end of which time everyone in the room but two women took off all of their clothes.

One of the clothed women standing near me said, "Now what do I do? How can I possibly get my clothes off?" I just very quietly said "take them off," which she did. The simplicity and quietness of my request seemed to release her from her former resistance. In the meantime, the other one made quite a fuss but finally got her clothes off. We then walked around and looked and touched one another and gradually got used to the nudity.

On my previous trips to Esalen I had been exposed to nudity in the baths. I was not particularly reluctant to take my clothes off under these other circumstances. I had long ago learned the lesson that groups of people in the nude had an ethic and a politeness that is probably even greater and more restricting than when they are dressed. I had also learned that practically everyone is self-conscious about his body, and that most people do not like the way their bodies look. I was no exception.

During the next week, I was in a workshop led by Steve Stroud with John Heider (two group leaders) in the wings. Steve was running a very intensive encounter group. This was my first exposure to the high-energy-level encounter. Steve definitely did not believe in discussing verbally ("head-tripping") at any great length. He believed in using nonverbal communication at a high emotional level. At one point during the week, I learned another fundamental lesson.

In the group was Steve's brother, Bill, who had just returned from Vietnam. There was a bit of rivalry going on between Bill and Steve as to which one of them was running the workshop. During the previous week Bill had finished a workshop with John Heider. Bill was trying to use Heider's techniques in the Stroud workshop. This led finally to Steve challenging Bill as to who was the leader.

In the resulting discussion, a young wrestler from Cornell joined in with Bill and Steve in their leadership discussion. They finally decided to wrestle, first Bill and Steve, and then the winner would wrestle the Cornell wrestler. About this point I got rather impatient, and at the same time a bit excited, and shouted at them, "When you guys have finally decided who the wrestling champ is, then we can get on with the work of this workshop." The immediate answer was, "Oh, so you need to fight too," from Steve. I denied this vehemently, but they insisted. After Bill and Steve had finished wrestling, and the young wrestler had finished wrestling Steve, then it was my turn. I was to wrestle the Cornell wrestler.

I went into that encounter extremely frightened. Basically, I was afraid of either killing or being killed. My overreaction to the situation brought out a fixation carried over from childhood. I was afraid of rage, afraid of getting into the rage space, the red rage space.

When I was 8 years old, my older brother had provoked me. We had provoked one another, really, to the point where I went into the red rage space. I threw a toy cannon at him just missing his head. Suddenly, I realized that I had attempted to kill him, and that if the cannon had been an inch closer I might easily have done so. At that instant I decided never to lose my temper again. The computer became fixated against this forbidden rage space.

We proceeded to wrestle with all of the careful controls around the wrestling match that are set up in Steve's encounter groups: staying on the mat, having people between us and the windows, the walls and the doors so that we wouldn't get hurt, and staying on our knees, never really standing up and not using fists. We agreed to abide by the rules. Before we started, Steve asked each of us to tell what he could give the other one in this battle. I said I could give some understanding and wisdom to the younger man, and he said he could give me youth and strength. We then proceeded to wrestle.

I was desperately afraid and hence was working extremely hard and was wearing myself out very rapidly. He was much more relaxed and proceeded to wrestle in a typical college wrestler fashion following the rules. In my desperate state I automatically did a judo hold on his arm just when he thought that he had me pinned. I held his arm strongly enough so that he gave up, very surprised, and so was I.

There had been nothing in the rules about avoiding using what one knew such as judo and jiujitsu, which I had learned in college. I immediately went onto a high in the tremendous release of that inhibitory program against the rage space, because now I felt competent to deal with my high-energy aggressive emotion. I realized that there is a whole spectrum of reactions to one's rage which aren't necessarily killing. I was released from the fixation put in at eight years of age.

I thanked the Cornell wrestler and Steve for a very profound change in my deepest nature. During this week I saw many profound changes in many people. For example, there was the little housewife from Florida in her first encounter group. She was Catholic, had five children, was forty-five years old, and turned out to be very talented in a very special region of human activity. She could go into trance automatically.

I discovered this in the middle of an encounter group in which somebody became extremely angry with her; she sat there in the middle of the floor unmoving and kind of disappeared. Her body was there, but obviously her mind wasn't. I immediately picked up the fact that she went into trance when frightened.

Steve had us get together in dyads (two-somes) outside the hours for group work, and in the next dyad encounter with her I asked her if she knew what she was doing. She described it very accurately. She said that when she gets frightened, she goes down inside into a small grey place by means of looking at any bright object across the room. She fixes her gaze on the bright object and then jumps out of her body into this small grey place. I found this a very fascinating maneuver and asked her if she could reproduce it for me. She tried but couldn't do it. I said, "apparently you have to be frightened to do this." That was the clue.

I managed to get her frightened enough so that she could do it. While she was in the trance, I suggested that there were other ways of handling her fear and her anger. I talked to her in her little grey place. She trusted me. We arranged for a set of steps out of the little grey place, ten steps rather than one big jump; I said, "As you come out of trance you will move up the steps toward the usual consensus reality. On the way you will take a trip into the universe and find out what's on all of these other steps."

This she agreed to do and started up. She stayed out of her body, traveled out into the universe, came back onto this planet, came back into the baths, and into her body. We repeated this several times, and she walked down the steps and came back up the steps several times.

This all took about three days. On the fourth day, back with the encounter group, she allowed herself to become angry at a great big man who was very sophisticated in encounter, and hence wasn't moving at all. She decided that he was going to move. She worked up her rage, ran across the room and butted him in the stomach with her head, knocking him flat. She then proceeded to stay with him and to comfort him, to care for him and to work like a Trojan with the rest of the group in getting him to move. This was a really fantastic advance for her, to be able to ride on her fear energy and her anger energy and then do effective work with a person rather than jumping into trance and leaving her body. During that week we discovered two other people who were doing similar kinds of things in threatening situations. Apparently, to go into trance to escape the consequences of what's going on outside is a fairly common, civilized reaction to rage or fear.

The week following the Stroud encounter group, I was in a Fritz Perl's weekend and week-long workshop of Gestalt therapy.

Fritz was the originator and the old master in Gestalt therapy. The group that he was working with sat around the sides of the room on chairs. Beside him there was a chair called the "hot seat." If one wanted to "work with him," one got into the hot seat beside Fritz. I watched some of the more experienced people get into the hot seat and watched what happened once they were there before I tried it myself. I began to see that one dived into painful or other negative places that one did not like to enter and let Fritz do the programming once one was into the emotional space. This was my version at that time of the basis for working with Fritz.

The first thing that I wanted to work on was a problem that I had had continually most of my professional life, what I called "me and my audience." In this mode of operation of my biocomputer, I was in the middle of a group inside my head. I spoke to this group, my audience, and expected them to react in certain ways. I carried out what I later called a TV script having to do with my audience. This to me was a time-wasting and energy-wasting game that I was playing inside my own head.

When I got in the hot seat I told Fritz this was my problem. He said, "All right, put your audience in that chair, and you stay in your chair. Now talk to your audience." I said, "Why are you always there? Why do you bother me? Why do you sit there watching and listening? Why don't I get any responses from you? Why don't I get the responses that I want, that I need from you? Are you real? What do I need you for? Go away. I'm angry with you."

Fritz said "Okay, now get in the other chair and be the audience and tell John what you think of him." So as the audience I said, "You are a posturing fool. You stand up there and lecture us. You tell us what makes the world go around. You tell us what makes you operate. You are such a great analyzer, and yet here we are. Here we sit, watching all of this, criticizing you and you really don't know what it is all about. You are an egotistical fanatic playing the game of science, whereas you really don't know what's happening. You can't understand us. You can't understand why we're in your head. You don't even know how to get rid of us."

Fritz said, "Okay, shift." So I got back in my chair and became John again. By this time I was very angry, as John, and I said to the audience, "God damn you. I've had Enough of your back talk. You guys are really me in disguise. I know what you're doing. You are splitting me up into tiny little control systems." Then I shouted "Fuck you!" Fritz then said "Do to the audience what you would like to do to the audience." I raised my hands over my head, made fists and came down on the barrel that was the audience and smashed in the top of it with a great deal of satisfaction and rage. Fritz watched all this. He said, "How do you feel?" and I said, "Great."

He said "Now go around to the group and tell each one what you would really like to tell each one of them." I did so, giving each one a very personal message very much to the point about our relationship. This completely cleaned me out in regard to the audience for a while.

A few days later I got into the hot seat again, this time about the death of my mother. I had some unfinished business which caused a continuous tape loop, having to do with guilt about her death, to rotate below my levels of awareness. I had spent 7 years working to keep her alive, and then, at the end, when the cancer finally killed her through a respiratory death, I blamed myself for having kept her alive by artificial means for so long.

I got in the hot seat and Fritz said, "Okay, go back to your mother's death." I went back to that particular day and began to hear her dying, became frightened, and came back to the group. Fritz said, "Go back." I went back again and started going through the fear, the grief, and the guilt connected with the doctors, with my own part in it. I examined very carefully the whole tape having to do with her death. I cried. I became extremely fearful, got into panic, then I cried with grief again. Three times Fritz put me through it and finally he said, "Okay, you haven't quite finished with that but you have dealt with most of it." He let me off the hot seat.

I spent a total of two weeks and one weekend in his workshops and learned very much about myself and about others and about his technique. I was impressed with the fact that he could tune in on where one was and then program one to move even further into the space that one was reluctant to go into. I found that as long as one was willing to allow him to program one, and to go ahead into whatever it was, then Fritz was happy and one made progress.

I was next exposed to Ida Rolf for a week. I received my first three hours of what's called "Rolfing." Ida has worked out, over a forty-year period, a technique of working on deep muscles, the fascia, and the joints in such a way that structural integration is restored to one's body. One stands, walks, and does other things correctly the way one did as a child before trauma spoiled the line of the body. Ida frees up the body by stretching the fascia around the muscles. This leads to pain if one resists what she is doing or if the muscles themselves resist what she is doing.

During the first hour when she was working on my chest, I was resisting and experiencing intense pain. I saw her as a witch with a tall black hat and fangs. I told her this and she said, "I am merely a nice little gray-haired old lady. The pain is yours. I am not causing the pain. You are."

During that week I learned how one can tie up energy in muscle postures that hold the body in certain definite attitudes as a result of previous trauma in childhood, which function with brain feedback repeating (like tape loops) for years.

For example, she was working on my left shoulder. Suddenly I saw myself at two and a half dragged across the lawn by my favorite collie dog who had his teeth gripping my left shoulder. I was in panic and rage, and I had a sense of being betrayed by my favorite dog. Suddenly, as the adult, I could see more of the scene, and I saw the dog had been dragging me away from a wall that I had been about to fall over. Suddenly I was able to forgive the dog and accept the pain, and as she continued to work on the shoulder there was no more pain.

Thus I realized that the human biocomputer includes the muscle systems, and the way these are held by central nervous system patterns of activity is a function of fixation in childhood. Trauma causes hiding of the causes of the trauma, thus setting up a tape loop in the central nervous system, which goes on perpetually activated until broken into either at the brain end or at the muscle end.

When Ida goes into such an area, she finds the muscles that are tense and presses on them very strongly, stretching the fascia. This causes pain, which then reorganizes the central nervous system for that area, thus breaking the loop. It was with an intense sense of relief that I gave up the tension in that left shoulder, tension that I did not even know that I had.

Ida showed that she had an eye, a sensitive pattern recognition system, for such evidences of trauma. She could look at somebody's body and feel it and tell immediately where these spots were and where these systems were. I suddenly began to realize that one did not have to go down into old age and become arthritic, that with Rolfing one could stay youthful. At that time Fritz Perls at seventy-five had had fifty hours of Rolfing and showed it in his youthful, bouncy step.

Through Rolfing I also discovered some other important properties of the human biocomputer. When I was twenty one I was in the woods near Klamath Falls, Oregon, working on a survey crew. I was the chief brush cutter. In cutting a path for the survey crew through a swamp, the ax had slipped on a wet root in the swamp and had gone into my foot, cutting it deeply. I didn't know that I had cut myself. I thought that I had cut the little dog that belonged to the head of the survey crew, when I saw the blood spurting up from the leaves below. I couldn't see my own foot. There was no pain, but suddenly I realized that I had cut myself. I lay down, raised my leg up in the air and shouted for the survey crew. They came and took me off to the hospital where the doctor sewed the cut from the bottom up in multiple layers. It became infected and I had to spend twelve days in the hospital.

During the week of the Rolfing, Peter Melchior had started to work on my feet and came across this scar. I warned him that this was a peculiar place on my foot where the nerve fibers grew in a peculiar fashion and it was extremely sensitive. He said, "Okay," and approached it rather carefully. We were working in a room high on a cliff above the Pacific Ocean. At the instant that he started to put his fingers through the scar on my foot a jet plane came by the cliff. The noise of the jet went from my foot to my head at the instant he traveled through the scar, so there was fantastic energy release from the scar. The noise of the jet ran that energy from my foot all the way to my head and out the top of my head. During this, I saw the ax descending over my foot and very slowly cutting the skin, the first layer of subcutaneous tissue, the fascia, the ligaments, and going on down into the bone. This time I felt the pain of the entrance of the ax, which was missing in the original happening. As he continued to work on it, I also felt the pain of the surgeon stitching it up. (Peter reported that he thought I had made the noise, not a jet.)

Suddenly, I realized that I had blocked the pain in the original experience. This scar had held the potential of that pain ever since. It also had a basic traumatic memory, a tape loop attached to it. I had favored that foot, favored that region of the foot, and had not completed the hole that was left in my body image here. The Rolfing allowed this hole to fill in, allowed my posture to improve in respect to that foot, and the realization of the pain passed away.

In the midst of these rather intensive workshops that I was taking from others, I gave a weekend workshop of my own. This was my first experience with the workshop way of presenting material to a group. There were two hour sessions scheduled Friday night, Saturday morning, Saturday afternoon, Saturday night, and Sunday morning.

My previous experience had been with lectures rather than with workshops. The difference lies in the fact that in a workshop one participates with the audience. The audience is on the same level with the leader, and it expects direct experience rather than being lectured at. Before the workshop started, I had had a lot of doubts and fears about my ability to do this. It was all very new to me, and it was a very large change from participant to leader.

I had been very busy at Esalen changing my whole attitude toward my previous life and dropping my previous identity insofar as I could do this. When I was approached at Esalen as "the John Lilly who had worked with dolphins," I found this to be a "downer" and I resented the interruption of my change of identity by bringing up an older identity. The scheduled workshop was on "us and dolphins," thereby reinvigorating the old image with which I currently was uncomfortable.

In the first session, I told the participants that I would give a lecture and would answer questions about dolphins only on Friday night. The rest of the sessions would be devoted to their finding out by firsthand experience what it is like to be a dolphin insofar as they were capable of doing this.

One participant, a psychiatrist from Los Angeles, objected to this strenuously, saying he did not expect that this weekend was going to be an encounter. I said, "Let's wait and see." He did stay.

The first evening I gave a lecture about dolphins with audience questions interspersed. As I promised, the rest of the workshop was devoted to firsthand experience as to what it would be like to be a dolphin. I pointed out that human beings are land animals, featherless bipeds with hands, who wear clothes and make things, and who cannot swim very fast. For a human to appreciate the position of the dolphin at sea, he must understand their breathing programs and the necessity of having only a voluntary respiration when in the sea. This fact alone makes each dolphin dependent upon all other dolphins. There is a mutual interdependence, which is far greater than it is between human beings. If a dolphin, for any reason, becomes unconscious, he stops breathing and sinks. His only chance of survival is for his fellow dolphins to bring him to the surface and wake him up.

In the workshop I showed that in order to be like a dolphin, the members of the workshop must depend totally on one another. They must love one another, play with one another, and experience the dangers of swimming in water with one another.

In one session we used the baths at Esalen to illustrate the points. Each member of the workshop participating in this exercise hyperventilated until his consciousness changed while in the warm water. While he did this he was watched over by another member of the workshop. As he began to have various experiences because of the hyperventilation, he was aided by the other member in various ways, including being prevented from sinking. Each one took turns doing the exercise.

Previous to this exercise I had told them on dry land how to breathe like a dolphin. This is a good method of breathing for meditation. One lies on one's back, blows all of the air out of one's lungs and fills them to the fullest capacity and holds one's breath as long as one can. This quiets the respiration and allows one to do a meditation free of the respiratory movements. When one can't hold the air any longer, one blows all the air out very fast and sucks it in again very fast, in a very impulsive short fashion.

Practice of this on dry land is necessary before doing it in water. In the tanks, the participants lie on their backs and breathe in this way. As soon as one fills one's lungs completely, one is floating "on the air in the lungs." As one begins to run out of oxygen and the carbon dioxide accumulates, one blows all the air out as far as he can very rapidly and pulls the air in before one can sink. It is the rapid emptying and filling which prevents the body from sinking. One is nonbuoyant for such a brief period of time that one doesn't have time to sink.

This is a good safety maneuver if one is caught in the water after falling overboard for any reason. One can relax this way and recover one's strength and decide what one is going to do. It could be an excellent life-saving procedure.

One can close one's eyes and do this maneuver in the tank and do an in-the-water meditation, very much as one does in the physical isolation tank. Since there is water in one's ear against the ear drum, the sound intensity is very much reduced. If one clasps one's hands under the neck so that the elbows are out under the water, this assures not tipping over to the side. In water nineteen inches deep, one keeps one's feet on the bottom of the pool with the knees bent and the rest of the body straight. This is needed in fresh water as the lower body is not buoyant enough to support the feet and legs. However, in salt water (like the sea or that in the Great Salt Lake in Utah) there is a high enough buoyancy so this isn't needed and one can float at the surface totally.

With this kind of meditation position one can really "float off," out of one's body, and do various kinds of innerspace maneuvers that one cannot do without it, at least at the beginning. It is a very fast doorway to get one into the floating innerspaces. This is the technique that I used in St. Thomas in the tank using LSD in 1964-1966.

Working with this technique at Esalen without LSD, I was able to return into many of the spaces that I had achieved earlier. Several of the participants in the workshops moved into new spaces very rapidly. Some of the more talented persons who were capable of entering trance did so and achieved very far-out experiences. We had to insist that people not do this in the tanks without another participant or a staff member being present. Mounting enthusiasm could easily have led to an accident.

It is an unwritten law at Esalen that each participant that comes there takes responsibility for himself, for his own safety, and does not do things that he doesn't feel capable of doing. This is a necessary point of view to have since one is pushing one's self way beyond one's usual limits and taking risks that one doesn't normally take. It is absolutely necessary that one assume the responsibility for one's ability to take these risks. Fritz called it "response ability." I had been through some of this risk taking myself, and I asked the participants in this workshop to do the same.

Other aspects of the workshop touched upon were that the dolphins were close, that they had a freely moving and joyful life constantly together, and that they had no compunctions about bowel movements, urination, or their sex life. I intimated that humans could well afford to try this way of living. Some people had successfully achieved this with a good deal more of "divine objective love" in their relationships and with that sort of dispassionate directness that one found among the dolphins. If we would love one another, whether the other person liked it or not, I felt that we could get farther along on our spiritual trip. Today, I still feel that by emulation of the dolphins' ways we could make a lot faster progress in loving one another, and in enjoying life, and abolishing the tensions that go on between groups of people. I hope that during the next ten years we can achieve this. When we begin to get enough people into this space, then maybe we'll be ready to return to the dolphins.

Several of the staff at Esalen were in the workshop and later expressed their enthusiasm for what had been presented, and for what they had experienced. Most of my fears were abolished as the workshop progressed. I saw how much people really wanted to know about dolphins and about themselves. From that point on, I had no more problems being a leader of workshops, at least no problems within myself. I had begun to see the ways and means of having people experience new and novel experiences with a new format. I presented the human biocomputer set of concepts and ways of dealing with one's self as an aid to navigating inner space. In that first workshop, I saw a great potentiality for presenting that point of view in future workshops.

Chapter 6
ANOTHER LOOK AT MYSTICISM

Since I'd been through an extremely intensive six weeks of workshops at Esalen, I was a bit tired and decided to rest at Gorda Ranch. In the workshops, I had not found what I had been hunting for. I had not found any help in my search for explanations of, or further accesses to, spaces I'd learned about in the isolation tank experiments with LSD. I had found new spaces having to do with the planetside trip with the help of Fritz Perls and other leaders at Esalen. The missing part was beyond the limits that the Esalen group put on their own experiences, in the then current emphasis on the "here and now," and on doing a better job of the planetside trip. In the workshops I took, the mystical side was left out.

Then a coincidence occurred that helped me to move more freely in the direction I was seeking. Baba Ram Dass arrived at the ranch for a six-week stay. I met him there for the first time. I had heard of him as the Harvard psychologist Dick Alpert, who in the early days of LSD had worked with Timothy Leary until both of them were expelled from Harvard for their drug experiments. Dick was someone who had been through the drug scene, who had then gone to India and spent a year with a guru, studying Yoga, and returned to the United States as Baba Ram Dass. He had been through most of the severe disciplines of Yoga, pursuing the Ashtanga or eight-limbed Yoga. He had lived in rather severe conditions in his own small hut, bathing every morning in an icy cold mountain stream and spending most of his days doing the exercises assigned by his guru.

From Ram Dass's example and from watching him teach, I received a lot of first-hand information about Yoga. He introduced me to the writings of Patanjali, who presented the basic Yoga assumptions in 196 simple statements (sutras) written about the time of Aristotle (400 B.C.). During the next few weeks, I obtained ten different translations of Patanjali, including two giving the original Sanskrit. The most useful of these was *The Science of Yoga** by I. K. Taimni. Taimni is a biochemist in India who has been studying Yoga for forty years.

I began my first sorties into the various types of meditation. I tried the concentration/contemplation/samyama-type exercises from Patanjali. In these exercises, one concentrates upon a single object, either outside oneself or in one's mind, long enough and intently enough so that one finally fuses with the object and the "see-er" fuses with the "seen." I had also been reading Ramana Maharishi and his directions, in which he said to meditate on the question, "Who am I?" One answer is, "I am not the see-er, I am not the seen." Following the directions of Patanjali, and the leads that I had laid out in *The Human Biocomputer*, I found a further extension of the meditation exercise.

---

* Wheaton, Ill.: Quest paperback, Theosophical Pub., 1967.

The new, more expanded meditation went as follows: "My brain is a huge biocomputer. I am the self metaprogrammer in this biocomputer. The brain is housed in a body. The mind is the software of the computer." These are the basic assumptions put forth in *The Human Biocomputer*. The key to the meditation was "Who am I?" Answer: "I am not my body, I am not my brain, I am not my mind; I am not my opinion of me."

Later, this was to be expanded into the more powerful five-part meditation, "I am not the biocomputer. I am not the programmer. I am not the programming. I am not the programmed. I am not the program." When the meditation had progressed to the latter point, I suddenly was able to break loose from the biocomputer, the programmer, the programming, the program, and the programmed and sit aside – from my mind, from my brain, from my body – and watch them operate and exist separately from me.

Thus, for me, Patanjali was expanded and rephrased into a more modern terminology. The old "see-er" was part of the programmer, the old "seen" was one of a series of programs. There was some overlap between the concepts, but the new concept included far more than the old one did. That which is programmed and the programming process itself were not represented in the Patanjali forms. Other meditations from other writers such as "watching one's thoughts go by, watching the thinking process, and watching the thinker" would be a closer yet incomplete approximation of the new point of view. The programming view (metaprogramming) is a far more powerful point of view than any of the older ones. It has the advantage of being constructible in modern computers for further study. It is also readily teachable to those who know something of computers and computer programming. Having experienced several workshops and having given several workshops, I went on and wrote a series of metaprograms in blank verse that summarized where I was at that time and where I wanted to be in the future. I dictated these on a hillside above Gorda Ranch early one morning after dawn, while the birds were singing in that inspiring Big Sur setting. The rest of this chapter gives the metaprograms of the summer of 1969.

Of Mountains and Molehills

"Where there's a mountain, there must be a molehill under there somewhere."

–John Hammontree of Big Sur

Often one has the feeling of climbing a mountain, for weeks, months, years; later one finds it was only a molehill. One was crawling along the level ground; the steep slope was only imagined. One was creating the steep slope. The mountain was one's own imaginings, one's own work directives.

We make work of our life to seem virtuous to ourself; blaming others and circumstances of money and of culture. One's pride, vanity, and the precious opinion of what one is and of what one is becoming, through mountain climbing, creates the mountain slope.

"Look at me – look at how far I've climbed up the mountain! I'm higher than you are. If you're higher than I am, I started lower than you did and have really climbed further. My mountain is steepest."

To see that all mountains are small molehills, that all human climbing is the delusion of a dream, move into planetary orbit, and looking down, see that all mountains are molehills. Move up and away from thyself.

Look back down the past of thyself. There are no mountains, no molehills. There is only a dream of past encounters, illusions of past strivings, dream slopes of dreamt opposition. In storage there is nothing but recordings of crawlings on the face of one small planet.

So why not enjoy bliss and ecstasy while still a passenger in this body, on this spacecraft? Dictate thine own terms as passenger. The transport company has a few rules, but it may be that we dream up the company and its rules too.

There is only internal peace, internal bliss, internal transforms of everything into joy, in the one place one really lives. There are no mountains, no molehills… just a central core of me and transcendent bliss.

Beyond Vanity

When I look back into my apparent past life, I find faulty recordings in my mind. I made records; rather something made records – probably very good ones.

I fought the recordings, edited them to fit my expectations of me, vain in my pride of me; I created "the false image of me." I patched and repaired broken me, yet I was never broken – never repaired – only this image of me. All my work was illusory. The repair bench, the image, was imagined.

I have always been me, always will be me. The true recordings are there if I want to feel-experience them as they really happened: But why look back into nonexistence, into old files long past? Only to look back and know that something did a good job of recording? Recording what?

The future of me – is there any without fright, pain, grief? Without further editing, repair, false recording? Is this all I do… juggle a truth into falsity? Is this the work for this trip?

I lay the recordings of falseness alongside the true recordings. I compare the two. I suffer in the comparison. Why?

I value too much the image of me that I raised too high. In the comparison, big image becomes little man. Little man suffers. The "big me" is a repeat of an old recording of treating records falsely. Falsifying the little; making it big and imagining it big.

Here and now and in the future heres and nows, I hear and I know, I heres and I nows – then.

Something else made the good recordings I edited. Why not let me make good recordings by resigning as editor/repairman? Let me be just me – hereing and nowing – accepting what is, and what is not, equally, as true.

Beyond me is much I haven't even imagined. It has always been beyond me. Here's the joyful pursuit, beyond here and now, to infinity, to the nullity of the creative Void.

Inspection of Expectations – Cata- and Ana-strophic

I expect thee, I expect thee to do, I expect thee to be – what?

Thou expectest me, thou expectest me to do, thou expectest me to be – what?

I expect them, I expect them to do, I expect them to be what?

I expect, thou expectest, what?

I expect, they expect, what?

I expect, thou expectest, they expect, what?

When thou expectest I expect thee to expect what they expect – I ask, why expect?

I answer, because I expect too.

I am here to live up to my expectations of me; am I?

But, what are my expectations of me?

They expect me to ———— . Do they?

Do they really care? Thou expectest me to ———— . Doest thou?

Doest thou really expect, care?

Care for expectations?

Expecting to persist in past patterns? Mine, thine, theirs?

Expecting to search? Search for new patterns? New expectations?

Expecting to strive? Strive for escape from expectations?

Expecting to evade old expectations? Of me, of thee, of them?

I expect my expectations are the expectations of others, not mine.

I imagine what thine expectations are. And assume they are mine.

I expect what I write of expectations, I expect that when I write of expecting is read, it will start expectations of me, in thee and them.

I search, I write, expecting further expecting. Why search, why write, why expect? Why thee? Why them?

Why me?

Great Men, Expectation, Meditation, Love, and Levitation

Is there really such a thing as a great man?

Are we not all microbes on a mud-ball rotating around a Type-G star two-thirds of the way from galactic center to the indefinite edge, in one small galaxy in the universe of galaxies – so what is a great man, what is a messiah, an avatar, an enlightened one?

In the microbe's imagination, there is a theory that he is not a microbe. His theory says, "There are beings, greater than I, of which I am a part. All I must do is realize my true self, see my soul, realize my Atman, join Universal Mind, become one with God, be spread throughout the Universe, tune in on the Infinite, transform the clay to the Divine, live and think right, and join God and the Angels."

Of course, since he is only a microbe on a mud-ball, why not have fun with the supergame, Microbial?

A group of microbes say to one another, "We are great. We have found a great man. The great man tells us how to realize our true nature, how to be enlightened. He tells us we are each great and He will show us the way to shed microbial illusions of being a microbe."

"Join up – here's the path, follow my lead – I have the Truth – but you must have discipline – my discipline. The Universal Law, through me, is revealed. Expectate, through me. Meditate – here's how. Love and levitate, as I did."

To Believe in Something

The something to believe in – somehow, somewhere, within inner space or without, in outer space – the existence theorem, "It Exists," must be positive and whole.

From where oneself is now, one believes that one can get belief in something by some way, route, program.

If the way, route, program is seen to include changes in self, then one more belief is that one can change. One changes to believe in something.

The search for the something cannot be done before belief that something exists. Something to believe in. The something to believe in, is greater, somehow, than one's present self. It, something, can be future self, changed.

It can be something, or someone human outside oneself. It can be something out there, among the planets, the stars. It can be something everywhere... inside and outside. Something far beyond Man. Something you learn from and communicate with. Belief in something – concentrated, purposeful, determined – comes hard. Once believing in something beyond oneself, then it comes more easily.

Bhakti Karma

To get to our thing let us speak in the dyad, us.

I have my thing, you have your thing, we have our thing.

Our thing is not mine, is not yours; our thing is ours. I know my thing, you know your thing, we know our thing.

You do not know my thing, I do not know your thing.

I know my part of our thing, you know your part of our thing, our thing exists only in us.

With no us, there is no our thing. We are our thing… only us.

To get beyond our thing, beyond us, let us speak of Them beyond us.

Imagine a human being, beyond you, beyond me.

Imagine a nonhuman being beyond a human being.

Imagine a being beyond that nonhuman being.

Imagine God beyond all beings, yet all beings and being itself.

To get back to our thing – to us.

To the little boy in me, I am a God, you are a Goddess.

To the little girl in you, you are a Goddess, I am a God.

To the God in me, I am a little boy, to the Goddess in you.

To the Goddess in you, you are a little girl, to the God in me.

To God, we are two little beings, dreaming of Him.

To God, we are an extension of His being, little ones.

So we are all One, in God. Our thing is part of Him; our small part.

To get back to us, the little boy loves the little girl loves the little boy.

The God loves the Goddess, loves the God.

I love you love me, in God, we love.

Jnana – Stage I

I don't have to understand – I know they run the Universe, and they run me.

No matter my opinion of their job; good or bad, they keep on doing it. They do the job assigned them by those above them.

So I do the job they assign me.

When necessary, they tell me.

I listen to them, I ask them. They hear me, they help me.

Jnana-Stage II

I am thee, thou art me, we are One. I love me, love thee, love the One.

Thou lovest thee, lovest me, lovest the One.

The One loves us.

Jnana-Stage III

I am them, thou art them, I, thou, they are One.

I love them, love thee, love the One.

Thou lovest them, lovest me, lovest thee, lovest the One.

The One loves All.

Jnana-Stage IV

Thou art me, they are me, they thou I are One.

They love thee, love me, love the One.

The One loves them, loves us.

The One is Love.

Limits of Belief Transcended

At first one's limits are set by the belief "I am centered in my physical brain." (That which one believes to be true, is true, or becomes true, at first within limits to be found experimentally. These limits, themselves, are beliefs to be transcended.)

I am not limited by the known physical senses, known physical signals sent/received by my brain. (Transcended, these limits are left behind. I send/receive messages by means unknown with unknown entities greater than me.)

Beyond transcendence is an infinite variety of unknowns. (I move from my brain into other universes and spaces, other states of being. Once lived, these unknowns are no longer unknown.)

In the other universes and spaces, the other states of being, are teachers, guardians. (Beyond these unknowns, now known, is full complete Truth.)

The guardians/teachers make me aware, help me be aware, and help me to experience, when I'm ready, realities beyond belief, beyond proof, beyond demonstration, beyond theory, beyond imagination. (Beyond that Truth, full and complete, are unknowns.)

The teachers' teachers take over my lessons. (New unknowns become known. The cycle repeats. Mastered, these unknowns are transcended.)

Sutra I, Book Four, Patanjali

Perfections proceed from birth, or from light – containing herbs or from mantra, or from self-discipline, or from Samadhi.

The Guyatri Mantra

Om, the earthly atmospheric and celestial spheres, let us contemplate the wondrous solar spirit of the Divine Creator. May he direct our minds. Om.

Brahma Guyatri Shastra

May we know the supreme spirit. Let us contemplate the supreme reality and may that Brahman direct us.

Chapter 7
MORE MYSTICISM: MENTATIONS

In September, 1969, I started a fellowship at the Center For Advanced Study in the Behavioral Sciences at Palo Alto, California. The intent here was to give me sufficient time and secretarial facilities to write a book. I somehow felt the book would be connected with my studies of Patanjali and whatever came out of those studies. The beginnings of the present book resulted from that fellowship.

While I was at the Center, my friend, Dr. Lawrence Kubie, wrote me that a mutual friend of ours had lost a son because of LSD. The story was that the son had been visiting at another college and had been found dead at the bottom of a balcony. Analysis of his blood showed LSD in it. This brought home something that I had already known; that many parents did not understand, nor would they try to understand their children's problems, especially those having to do with drugs. In an almost militant fashion, they avoided investigating the effects of LSD. The literature and first-hand accounts are readily available to parents, but they are so wrapped up in the national negative program on LSD that they cannot see the realities behind this programming. Meanwhile, the young people of the country have taken up LSD with a great deal of enthusiasm and were proselytizing their friends.

Thus came my resolve to write a book and to do what I could to help parents and the youngsters understand one another and to understand LSD and other trips from the positive, the negative, and the objective viewpoints.

At one point during the fellowship, I had nearly completed the book. I put it aside for awhile to reconsider it. Several months later, upon reading it again, I decided to throw away everything except the first three chapters.

During the summer and fall of 1969 I heard from Claudio Naranjo, a West Coast psychiatrist with considerable background in mystical disciplines and a staff member of Esalen, about a "Sufi" in Chile by the name of Oscar Ichazo. Claudio went to Chile and worked with Oscar for two months, October and November of 1969. When he returned in January 1, 1970, we were all very curious as to what had taken place. It turned out that Oscar was willing to take a group of fifty Americans for a ten-month training period beginning July 1, 1970.

Before making up my own mind as to what I wanted to do in regard to such training, I wanted to see what had happened to Claudio. He had written me a letter saying that Oscar had got him into spaces that he'd never been in before, spaces that he found to be very desirable places. In fact, he had wanted to stay there and Oscar had asked him to come back out of those spaces.

This sounded so much to me like the spaces that I had got into with LSD and the isolation tank in the Virgin Islands that I became rather intrigued. It appeared that here was a man who was capable of showing one how to move into new spaces, without the tank, without LSD. I had experienced two of these spaces. I called them the Messiah Space and the Missionary Space. At that time, I had realized that I had come upon very deep and basic truths about realities that are not ordinarily experienced. In the first flush of ecstatic enthusiasm, I had felt that I must proclaim these to the world and show people how to get to these spaces. I felt that it was important for the future of world progress that everyone be able to attain these states and share them with others.

The only thing that had prevented me from becoming a Messiah or a Missionary had been my own scientific exploratory motivations, which would not allow such a use of the knowledge.

I could not be a dispassionate explorer and at the same time proclaim the benefits of the territory I'd found. It seemed to me that there was room for only one role – that of explorer, in the scientific sense. If I did anything else, including teaching, it would prejudice what I had found in the explorations. At that time, my main ambition was to maintain a dispassionate and objective point of view. I wrote this up in a small volume entitled *Programming and Metaprogramming in the Human Biocomputer.* *

To learn more about Oscar's methods, I did some of the group work with Claudio.

In that group work based on Ichazo's program as interpreted

---

* Reprinted 1970 by Portola Institute, Whole Earth Catalog Division, Menlo Park, Calif.

by Claudio, I had been taught mentations, some mantras, and some prayers. I pursued the mentations further and began using them and teaching them in my workshops. They have turned out to be an aid in terms of one's own thinking and in terms of teaching. They can be an open doorway into special new spaces once one learns them thoroughly enough to use rapidly.

In the mentations one places one's consciousness plus a specific idea in a specific part of one's body as follows:

In one's ears place the idea of substance (the unique objective reality of something, such as a person's substance) in eyes the form; in nose, one's possibilities (alternatives); in the mouth, one's needs; in chest, one's impulse (automatic energies); in upper belly, one's assimilation process; in lower belly, one's elimination process; in the genitals, one's orientation (either toward evolution or toward regression); in upper legs and upper arms, one's capacity; in knees and elbows; one's charisma; in the lower legs and lower arms, one's means; in the feet and hands, one's goals.

Once one is well acquainted with mentations, new areas in one's thinking can open up. If one is in trouble, or in doubt, or on a very negative bummer, one can use the mentations and discover pathways out into new places.

One metaprogram that I constantly remember is that the mentations must be available to be automatically entered into whenever there is a threat outside, whenever there is a need for reconsidering, whenever the space one is in is unpleasant and not wanted, whenever one conceives of a use for it. It is so automatic that when I am on a downer, I use the metaprogram.

When I get into the position of questioning the usefulness of the mentations, I start a series of mentations on the mentations themselves, thus getting into the metaprogramming position rather than getting involved in the "downer" programs or the "ego" programs coming from my biocomputer.

When I wanted to stop smoking in February, 1970, I used the mentations somewhat as follows: (Those of you who wish to stop smoking may find this a useful format to work with.)

Feet and Hands

"What are my goals in smoking?" (Pleasure and distraction.)

Lower Leg, Lower Arm

"What are the means to stop smoking?" (Stop.)

Knees and Elbows

"What is the relationship to others, my charisma, that keeps me smoking and that will allow me to stop smoking?" (Smokers vs. non-smokers.)

Upper Legs, Upper Arms

"Do I have the capacity to stop smoking?" (I stopped smoking once before for ten years so I do have the capacity to stop.)

Genitals

"What is my orientation in smoking?" (Obviously, it is toward destruction, through a temporary pleasure. My orientation in stopping smoking is toward further evolution of myself, increase of will power, increase of physical health.)

Lower Belly

"What must I eliminate in order to stop smoking?" (All of those programs connected with smoking.)

Upper Belly

"What must I assimilate in order to stop smoking?" (Some means of programming it out of my life and removing it as a real Program.)

Upper Chest

"What must I do to bring my impulses into line with not smoking?" (Eradicate the impulse to smoke, which is an artificial programmatic construct made up out of the pleasure of the smoke coming into my chest and the sensations therefrom – an artificial impulse.)

Mouth

"What do I need in terms of smoking and not smoking?" (The need, the taste in the mouth, is an artificial acquired habit and must be eliminated as an artificial need. The necessity of having cigarettes and of lighting them must be eliminated.)

Nose

"What are the other possibilities with respect to smoking?" (I have been smoking up to four packs a day. I have the possibility of future health without it. I might even take up the smoking of marjiuana. However, that would be substituting another need for this need. So, it is not a possibility.)

Eyes

"What is the form of smoking?" (The form of smoking is a very superficial thing... reaching for a cigarette, lighting it, inhaling deeply, and going on doing this, all day long.)

Ears

"What is the substance of smoking?" (It is a very poisonous toxic state. Smoking has nothing whatsoever to do with my own substance, with my own essence, and therefore, smoking must be eliminated.)

As a consequence of running the mentations, I set up the following little program, which prevented further smoking. When the impulse to smoke arose, I would go through (in my imagination) the process of taking the cigarette out of the pack, lighting it, inhaling deeply, enjoying the sensations thereof; but then I had to go on, and, in my imagination, continue smoking one cigarette after another until I realized the negative aspects of smoking... the punishment that existed *after* the reward. With this little by-play, which finally became a very short program lasting only a few seconds each time, I was able to completely *eliminate* the habit. So I stopped on February 14, 1970 – a triumph for the mentations.

About this same time, I was thinking of going to Chile and needed to learn some Spanish. So, through a delightful Argentinian by the name of Virginia Igonda, I learned my first Spanish sentences, "Fumar es muy malo. No fumar es muy bueno." I used these sentences as a mantram in addition to the other exercises given above.

Soon after this period, the four-month resident training period at Esalen began with me as a member. I was to receive resident training from other members of the staff at Esalen, and at the same time I was to do some teaching of the residents.

Chapter 8
GROUP WORKSHOP AT KAIROS

During my stay at Esalen I also gave a five-day workshop at Kairos, in Rancho Santa Fe, California, near San Diego. There were eighteen people of diverse backgrounds in this workshop, thirteen from the staff of Kairos and several from Esalen workshops that I had given previously. We had Kairos to ourselves, the whole Wishing Well Hotel in our control without interruptions from other groups for a full five days.

I had heard that Oscar Ichazo wanted everybody to be on a high protein diet for their work at the school. I agreed very highly with this choice.

The people who were working in the kitchen at Kairos were willing to cooperate. For five days we stayed on this diet of cheese, meat, eggs, fish and soybeans with one experimental meal of high carbohydrates.

I had first come upon this diet in 1936 as a student at Cal Tech in the biochemistry department under Dr. Henry Boorsook, whose main job at that point was setting up the minimum daily requirements for vitamins for the National Research Council. To find out what it was like to be in a protein-deprived state, I was put on a trial protein-free diet for a period of six weeks. It was a very low-energy state. We quickly determined that within twenty-four hours one was using up the protein in one's own body. Within two hours of taking outside protein, one shifted from one's own body proteins to the outside source. Later, when I was overweight, I also tried a pure protein diet; in six weeks I lost fifty pounds.

An adequate diet was designed for a Mt. Everest climbing expedition. Because of the specific dynamic action of protein, it was decided to make the Everest diet a very high-protein diet so as to have the necessary energy to withstand the cold and the constant activity.

Everyone in the group agreed to share what happened in periods outside of the actual group sessions – dreams and so forth. We started the first session with an intensive review of the goals of the group. It was agreed that we wanted to try to achieve an integration of each member of the group into the group insofar as this was possible.

The mentations were taught to the group in the first day or so. Many exercises using the mentations were brought in so that each member of the group knew the mentations thoroughly and made them part of himself. The goals in the mentations were set in advance for the group. Each person did the mentations on his own spiritual trip, the goal being to achieve a higher level than his own self, to reach the supraself level in his biocomputer. The mentations were also used as an exercise to develop the idea of the unknown in oneself.

Then the mentations were done in dyadic combinations. Two people would sit down opposite one another and go through the mentations, finding their goals as a pair, or a dyad. Dyadic goals were set at the metaprogram level so that each member would help the other within the dyad to achieve a higher state of consciousness so that a supraself for the dyad would be reached. Each person made a dyad with each other person until each person had formed seventeen dyads (the maximum possible since we had eighteen people). After this exercise was completed, everyone knew one another very well. All were motivated to move in the same direction.

The mentations were then done for group goals rather than dyadic or individual goals. The whole group was to move toward a group supraself... with a metaprogram for entities greater than the group to advise the group.

Using music as the prime stimulus, we brought in the auditions, an exercise in which parts of the *Bolero* are placed in each of the three centers: the movement center, the feeling center, and the thinking center. *Bolero*, according to Indries Shah and also according to Oscar Ichazo, is a Sufi piece of music composed by the Chusti group of Sufis to induce special states of consciousness. The medium range notes (the melody) are placed in the feeling center in the chest. The very high notes are placed in the thinking center in the head. The very low notes are placed in the movement center in the belly. Most of the group accomplished this exercise. Later they did a coordinated exercise involving the mentations and *Bolero*.

We went through Bolero several times with the mentation exercise. Fairly soon it took on new meanings that we had not previously detected in it. One's body began to change and one perceived new ways of thinking.

During the workshop we utilized a repeating tape loop of *cogitate*. We lay on the floor and listened to *cogitate* repeated once every three quarters of a second for a period of fifteen minutes. Each member of the group told the rest of the group what had happened to him. Most of the group heard alternate words to *cogitate*. Three insisted that the alternate words were on the tape. When they heard the accounts of other people and discovered that the other people heard words that were not on the tape, they were finally convinced that their own biocomputers had introduced these words. There was only one person with a fear reaction to the experience. This was relieved by discussing it with the rest of the group.

Other tape loops were used such as "deeper and deeper mother and I are fusing." Longer sentence length and fewer repetitions per minute necessitated more time to hear the variations projected into the sentence. There was also more time to go through psychological changes as a result of hearing the message at different levels. The message was a threat to both the men and the women in the room. Fusing with their biological mother was too much for them. Some persons changed the sentence so that it did not have the meaning of fusing with mother. It came out as "Keep her deep, her mother and I are fusing," thus keeping away from fusing with one's own mother, and instead, fusing with somebody else's mother.

The concept of the earth mother was used. It felt more secure to fuse with the earth mother than with one's own mother. As some fused with the cosmic mother, they became quite ecstatic.

Some people in the group made the sentence "Deeper and deeper, mother and I are fusing" into a law firm, "Deeper and Deeper, Mother and I," and the person would all fuse into a corporate entity. Because of this, they were able to "fuse" with the biological mother and were able to enjoy the trip very thoroughly. Those really fusing with the biological mother became at one with their real mother, realizing that they carried her in their head and that it was not the actual outside mother at all, but their own concept of their mother, which they had denied up to this point.

More and more of the group saw the point of this exercise, realized they had internal conflicts, and came to grips with them and the necessity of dealing with them. In group discussions, they found a lot of security in revealing these very peculiar inner programs that conflicted with one another. Using this technique, they were able to see very independent control systems (tape loops) buried down inside their computer, which at times would take them over without their permission.

As each individual began to open up to his own computer processes, in cooperation with the group, each became interlocked with the others present and shared operational data as to how his own biocomputer operated with other people. The structure of these processes began to become clear. Almost automatically, one became attached to other members of the group and shared more and more with them.

It is necessary for a kind of metaprogram to develop in the group as a whole in preparation for moving toward the supraself. One must be able to recast one's basic assumptions into a more open set of assumptions, a set that does not prohibit one from moving into new spaces.

I continued the presentation of my concepts of the human biocomputer and how it operates, including the supraself and supraspecies levels. I made the point that one's self, "I," "Me," is an entity in the biocomputer. For purposes of discussion, we call this entity the "self-metaprogrammer." It operates in a way that seems to be independent of the rest of the biocomputer insofar as this is possible. The entity that one speaks to in another person when one says "you" is also the entity that speaks when one says "I." These speaking entities occur in this fashion when one is consciously aware that this is the case. If one is consciously aware of his own processes, then one can say that the self-metaprogrammer is operating. There can be other independent control systems within the human biocomputer that take over and then the self-metaprogrammer seems to disappear. This can happen especially in high states of emotion and under special circumstances of stress. The self-metaprogrammer can abdicate and allow other systems to run the whole biocomputer. Then it is as if someone else (from the current environment or from the past) came into one's biocomputer and ran it. It is necessary, for progress in the spiritual sense, to be aware of these processes and to develop a respect for the unknown in one's self and in one's own biocomputer.

The next exercise was the "Beliefs Unlimited" exercise in which one attempted to move beyond one's current belief structures. We listened to a tape programmed in a repetitive fashion (5 presentations each time) to maximize absorption. The directions for listening to the tape were to lie in a comfortable position on the floor with the lights very dim and to just allow the metaprogramming to enter one's biocomputer.

Beliefs Unlimited

In the province of the mind, what one believes to be true either is true or becomes true within certain limits, to be found experientially and experimentally. These limits are beliefs to be transcended.

Hidden from one's self is a covert set of beliefs that control one's thinking, one's actions, and one's feelings.

The covert set of hidden beliefs is the limiting set of beliefs to be transcended.

To transcend one's limiting set, one establishes an open-ended set of beliefs about the unknown.

The unknown exists in one's goals for changing one's self, in the means for changing, in the use of others for the change, in one's capacity to change, in one's orientation toward change, in one's elimination of hindrances to change, in one's assimilation of the aids to change, in one's use of the impulse to change, in one's need for changing, in the possibilities of change, in the form of change itself, and in the substance of change and of changing.

The unknown exists in one's goals for changing one's self, in the means for that change, in the use of others in the changing, in one's capacity for changing one's self, in one's orientation toward changes, in the elimination of hindrances to changing, in one's assimilation of the aids to changing, in one's impulses toward changing one's self and undergoing changes, in one's needs for changes, in the possibilities for change, in the form of the changes themselves, and in the substance of the changes and of changing itself.

There are unknowns in my goals toward changing. There are unknowns in my means of changing. There are unknowns in my relations with others in changing. There are unknowns in my capacity for changing. There are unknowns in my orientation toward changing. There are unknowns in my assimilation of changes. There are unknowns in my needs for changing. There are unknowns in the possibilities of me changing. There are unknowns in the form into which changing will put me. There are unknowns in the substance of the changes that I will undergo, in my substance after changes.

My disbelief in all these unknowns is a limiting belief, preventing my transcending my limits. My disbelief in all these unknowns is a belief, a limiting belief, preventing my transcending my limits.

By allowing, there are no limits; no limits to thinking, no limits to feeling, no limits to movement. By allowing, there are no limits. There are no limits to thinking, no limits to feeling, no limits to movement.

That which is not allowed is forbidden. That which is allowed, exists. In allowing no limits, there are no limits. That which is forbidden is not allowed. That which is not allowed is forbidden. That which exists is allowed. That which is allowed, exists. In allowing no limits, there are no limits. That which is not allowed is forbidden. That which is forbidden is not allowed. That which is allowed, exists. That which exists is allowed. To allow no limits, there are no limits. No limits allowed, no limits exist.

In the province of the mind, what one believes to be true either is true or becomes true. In the province of the mind there are no limits. In the province of the mind, what one believes to be true is true or becomes true. There are no limits. (End of Beliefs Unlimited tape.)

The group was also given some ideas on how to move from one space into another. The process of moving from the space that I'm in now, which we will call "space number one," to a new space, "space number two," requires "space number two" to exist. So my first problem is to find "space number two" where I want to go.

I sit in "space one" and contemplate "space two." If the operation is successful, I suddenly find myself in "space two." "Space one" has been left behind. This shows that there is no barrier between "space one" and "space two," since, by definition, I have moved from one space to the other. No energy is required except that of concentration and contemplation.

However, I may be sitting in "space one" and be unable to contemplate "space two." In this case, there is a barrier between me and "space two" and no matter what anybody else tells me, I see this barrier and not the space. Instead of contemplating "space two," I contemplate the barrier. The barrier can be an ego program or an emotional state space or practically anything else that my biocomputer has constructed. The important point is that the barrier is something that I have constructed in the biocomputer. I must take the responsibility for the existence of that barrier. If I do not take that responsibility, the self-metaprogrammer cannot "debug" or deprogram that barrier.

As I sit and contemplate the barrier, I suddenly realize that there are several ways to get into "space two." One is to develop sufficient energy so that I can jump over the barrier. This can be done by arousing emotion, by taking LSD, by any of innumerable other techniques for piling up energy in the whole system. This technique enables me to enter "space two" at a very high energy level.

Another method is to see suddenly that the barrier has holes in it that come and go. If I move very fast, I can move through one of these "tunnels." This tunnel effect is true of all barriers, including the quantum mechanical barriers for electrons or other particles. In this method, I sit and contemplate the barrier until a tunnel appears through which I can go. This requires less energy than jumping over the barrier. However, it requires more energy than the first method of defining oneself in "space two" and then finding oneself there.

The above exercise was used to extend our abilities to move beyond our hidden beliefs. Barriers to movement consisted of a set of limiting beliefs that had to be transcended. Eventually one can move into supraself spaces by these techniques. Barriers to movement from one space to another in the supraself direction are called "ego programs" and are defined as that which keeps one out of Satori-Samadhi-supraself spaces.

The group at Kairos spent several hours in discussion and in practice of these ideas. They developed these ideas with specific examples of their experiences in the previous exercises of "Cogitate" and "Deeper and Deeper." Being more consciously aware of their own beliefs and of their manipulations of their beliefs, they began to loosen up and were able to travel into different spaces.

Chapter 9

GROUP RHYTHM AND GROUP RESONANCE AT THE KAIROS WORKSHOP

The major result of the group exercises was the tightening up of the group. Everyone had a much deeper regard for every other person in the group. There was a very deep sharing of experience and a realization that each person had far greater depth and height within them than was thought originally. The mutual appreciation and the developing love among the group members then led to some experiments that were later to be called *Resonance Within the Group*.

Resonance is an electrical engineering concept derived from radio and electromagnetic waves traveling in circuits. If one has a circuit that oscillates, an oscillator, one can feed energy from that circuit into spatially distributed circuits, such as wires running in parallel, as in cables, and then to tuned structures, such as a large antenna at the other end of the parallel wires or cable. By properly adjusting the electrical physical parameters of the system, such as capacitance or wire size, one can "detune" parts of the circuit to transmit the energy from one part to the other. For instance, a cable going from the oscillator to the antenna must be detuned in order to get maximum transfer of energy to the antenna.

The antenna itself must be tuned, that is, it must be adjusted in the length and its distance from the ground in such a way that one achieves a standing wave pattern on the antenna. The waves on the antenna itself, of voltage and current, must stand still, as it were, and not travel. When standing waves exist on the antenna, the oscillating field distributed over the antenna excites traveling waves in the surrounding space, which we call radio waves. The antenna then "radiates."

In the same way, a receiver of space waves radiated from an antenna must have a tuned antenna above the ground separated from surrounding objects and an untuned line going to the receiver to transfer the energy picked up in the resonating antenna at the proper frequency. The receiver is also tuned to the proper frequency. As one sets up these oscillators with their transmitting antennae and these receivers with their tuned receiving antennae, one can construct a communication network. At each location where the human receiver and transmitter is there must be electromagnetic transmitters and electromagnetic receivers of the familiar radio or television or F.M. varieties. A "tuning" of both the transmitting and receiving circuits to a resonance or maximum energy flow condition is necessary for optimum, undistorted communication on the channel.

I applied this reasoning to human groups. Presumably there are energies, to which each human is sensitive, that we cannot yet detect by means of our instruments. Built into our brains and our bodies are very sensitive tuneable receivers for energies that we do not yet know about in our science but that each one of us can detect under the proper circumstances and the proper state of mind. We can tune our nervous systems and bodies to receive these energies. We can also tune our brains and bodies to transmit these energies.

Presumably, there are many, many states of tuning for transmission and for reception. There are many, many bands of energy to which one can tune. There are bands emitted primarily by humans and received by humans. There are bands transmitted and received by nonhuman intelligences on this planet, which we may or may not be able to tune in on. There are bands transmitted and received by entities who are vastly larger than us and who reside in other parts of the galaxy. Some reception can be from planetary transmissions; some can be from stars, suns, dust clouds, and so forth; some can be from humanlike intelligence somewhere in the galaxy and some can be from apparatus constructed by civilizations a thousand to a million years more advanced in their science.

Some of these transmissions may be very noisy for us. We cannot possibly understand the message content so we will detect them as "noise" and attribute them to natural, passive sources such as moving atmospheres on planets. We will also say that things like "whistlers," which occur in our atmosphere and which are attributed to lightning strikes, have nothing to do with an intelligent transmission system.

As long as a system is beyond our comprehension, we will say that it is due to "natural causes." It may very well be that our atmosphere over the whole planet is part of an intelligence network whose code we have failed to break and whose transmissions are outside our present knowledge. It might be that if we could perceive the "whistlers" with the proper apparatus and the proper decoding procedures, we would find that it is a peculiar type of signaling between entities that, at the present time, we cannot understand. This is presumably what we mean by "natural causes." We put down anyone who tries to explain such happenings by means of processes operated by intelligent agents.

I explained these ideas to the Kairos Workshop group and hypothesized that, with the proper group activities, we could set up group circuits and then each individual would experience reception and transmission of new information. I hypothesized that if we could arrange the group in the proper physical configuration, we would resonate with some of these unknown energies and create new patterns of energy that each one of us could detect, and thus receive new and startling kinds of information. I further hypothesized that the conditions under which this would best be seen and detected by each one of us would be for us to get into resonance with one another in a physical arrangement in a room, so that we were a "resonating group circuit."

If there were the right number of people in the circuit, it would resonate; otherwise there would be traveling waves, and none of us would be able to detect them. Each person, then, is an element in an oscillating circuit and as one adds or subtracts elements, one reaches a resonant number of persons, each connected with the others. If one adds one more after one achieves resonance, the phenomena in the group should change to a moving wave rather than a standing wave, so the messages will not be as clearly received by each member of the group. Only repeating, standing wave oscillating messages will be detected unless a person is trained to pick up the nonrepeating traveling messages. The theory further proposes that an individual sitting in lotus or some other position, meditating, can bring himself into resonance with these energies and can receive messages from various entities, human and nonhuman, terrestrial and nonterrestrial, but this is more difficult than if the same person works in a group. The group tends to go toward resonance, closely coupling individuals and entraining them at the correct frequencies.

Further, a given individual may be better at transmission than other individuals. A given person may be a better receiver than a transmitter or a better transmitter than a receiver. These differences can be somewhat compensated for by putting the group in a circle. The powerful transmitting individuals are put at definite intervals. They can send throughout the circle and develop the standing wave pattern at high energy, thus bringing everybody above the threshold for detection.

Since we did not know the laws yet for group activity, nor how to arrange the group, we decided to allow it to happen. We would probably get some sort of direction below our levels of awareness (group entrainment in the cosmic network). If we were in the flow and allowed it to happen, it would probably happen correctly for the first time. Then we would have a problem figuring out what it was that we did correctly.

In my past experiences in the scientific lab work, I had generally found that to be the case. As one gets the inspiration for a new experiment, and does it, the experiment works. The scientist then spends several hundreds of hours and many weeks trying consciously to figure out what it was that he did correctly subconsciously in order to reproduce that first result.

We began the procedure by sensitizing and tuning ourselves to music. Everyone lay on the floor and listened to a tape recording of *Switched On Bach* done on the Moog Synthesizer. I had previously found, with groups, that this piece of music raised the individuals' energies, if each person allowed the music to flow through him. We then did an audition exercise with Bolero by Ravel, putting the high notes in the head, the melody in the chest, and the low notes in the belly.

After several hours of such preparation, we then formed a circle. Eighteen people chanced to be in the circle. The number of people coming and going had varied considerably during the week so it was coincidence that we had the eighteen which turned out to be exactly the right number of people for group resonance.

We did various kinds of things in the circle. First, we did mentations together as a group. Group mentations consist of concentrating our consciousness in our hands and feet for our group goals; in our forearms and forelegs for the group means; in our elbows and knees for our relationship to one another, our charisma. The group capacity was in the upper legs and upper arms. Group orientation was in the genital parts; group elimination in the lower belly; group assimilation in the upper belly; group impulse in the upper chest; group needs in the mouth; group possibilities in the nose; group form in the eyes; and group substance in the ears.

While we were doing this, we concentrated not on our individual body parts, but on the body parts of ourselves plus the body parts of everybody else in the circle. We then lay on our backs with our feet touching, the right foot touching the left foot of the adjacent partner and so on around the circle, with the feet toward the center of the circle. We held hands with the people on either side of us. Thus we set up the "real circuit" and the "programmed model circuit" in the group.

Bolero was turned on and we imagined the energy being transmitted from our left hand to our right hand around the whole circle – also from our left foot to our right foot. Each person put the music, according to the above mentation formula, into the proper place in his body. During the fifteen minutes of exposure to *Bolero,* everyone kept perfectly quiet in the dark. When the music was finished, we all sat up and we each reported our experiences to the group.

It turned out that as we went around the room and each person in turn reported his experience, the first six experiences were all different. The next six experiences resembled the first six and the final six resembled the other two groups of six. We discovered that every sixth person had the same experience, merely reported with a different vocabulary. This meant that in the circle, if one diagrams it, one can see that there are triangular groups of three, all of whom share an experience. This showed that there was a resonance structure that developed in the room with a series of waves that repeated themselves every sixth person.

There was a group of three that reported fantastic energy flows through their arms and legs coming in from left and going to the right. These three people were distributed on the points of an equilateral triangle. The next group of three reported seeing in the dark of the room a luminous energy flowing around the group. The next group of three reported a pillar of energy in the center of the group, building up in the dark and flowing out through the ceiling of the room. Of course, in the dark we could not see the ceiling. The next group of three reported seeing eighteen lights around the room. Apparently a light was above each person who was lying on the floor. The lights oscillated and changed color in time with the music. The fifth group of three saw distinct entities moving in a crowd through the room. Some of these were human, some were nonhuman, some were luminous, some were dark. The sixth group felt entities brushing through the group on the floor, but did not see them. They felt the presences without visualizing them.

As the information from each group was presented to the whole group, memories of additional things that had happened occurred within each group. For example those who had reported seeing the pillar of light in the center of the room felt that this pillar was an intelligent entity directing what was happening in the room. All of us became rather charged with what had happened. Some became intensely interested, some became a bit frightened, but everyone agreed that the experiment had worked.

Chapter 10
MY FIRST TRIP TO CHILE: OSCAR ICHAZO

Toward the end of the Esalen residence program, I began to feel that I should go down to Chile and meet Oscar Ichazo, to see what sort of a person he was, and to find out if I wanted to take the training. So in May I left the United States for Arica, Chile, for one week.

In that week with Oscar, I had found, for the first time on this planet, someone who apparently had been to the same spaces that I had been to, someone who could discuss these spaces intelligently and objectively and who at the same time could encourage me to accept my own experience as real. Our contacts were almost immediately "Essence to Essence."

Oscar's physical appearance on first sight does not live up to the visual expectation of a "holy man." He wears modern Western, stylish clothes in very good taste. His wardrobe is varied. He wears colored turtle-necks with trousers to match, a suit with shirt and tie when it is appropriate. He has special costumes for special rituals and ceremonies. Yet he dresses in such a way that he does not attract attention to himself. He uses color in his dress as an expression of the day's energy. He is of medium height, neither tall nor short. His black hair is cut relatively short and is thinning on top. He wears a mustache, black. He is balding. His eyes are of the darkest brown and prominent.

His features are very mobile when he expresses himself. One feels there is a genuine consciousness of feedback with other persons in face and body. There is the expert's economy of movement, of the use of his energy, in facial and bodily usage.

He has a repose, a meditative relaxing from which his movements originate. His speaking is similarly efficient and originates from a unified center within, reflecting the hearers' conscious center outside.

In experiencing his talks with other persons, I saw he apparently tuned in to where each one was and used language, tone, and content for that person's particular needs. With most of his communication he expresses the positive side, finding the positive in or behind the negative. Many times he showed me that my most negative (I thought) experiences were necessary teaching aids and hence positive. Many times he showed me that my temporarily negative viewpoint was just that, my own creation with no necessarily objective reality.

Experiences like these with Oscar showed me the usefulness of his basic thesis: achievement of desirable states of consciousness are partly matters of technique, empirically tested and proved by one's own experience.

At one point he introduced me to a dyadic eye fixation exercise, which is a powerful interpersonal programming technique. While sitting and not moving, each person looks into one eye of the other. When this is done for ten minutes to an hour or so, many things happen to oneself, one's perception, one's feeling, one's being.

In my first demonstration of this technique with Oscar, I seemed to go through shared past life experiences with him over several tens of lives in various parts of this planet, including China, Arabia, early Europe. Also, I went into spaces of great peace, quiet, and golden light. With Oscar all of these experiences were quite familiar, safe, and rewarding.

I spent a lot of time with Steve Stroud and Linda and Bob Jolly and Nancy, who were in training with Oscar. Oscar had told them that they could tell me all about what they were doing. He asked me not to transmit their information to the United States group that was coming down. He was experimenting with these four to find out those parts of his own training that were applicable to them. He was sort of using them as guinea pigs, as samples of North Americans and what sorts of things we needed in the training.

They demonstrated the Gym and the series of special physical exercises they were doing. They showed me some of the chants and mantras and they told me about their contacts with Oscar. At the time Oscar was doing a lot of individual work. Each student would take a tape recorder to each session and record everything that was said. They were on a fantastically intensive schedule at that time.

They would start at eight o'clock in the morning and would finish their school work at approximately midnight. They were having to take turns on the various household jobs such as obtaining food at the grocery stores and cooking. This was their only time off. They also told me about the desert exercises, the so-called "Pampas," done on Sundays.

During that week, I decided to come back in July. I left a good deal of the learning of this material until school started in July. I did not know how much this trial group of four had learned that Oscar would use with the new group, so it appeared wise not to go ahead at this point.

Continuing my own personal contact with Oscar, I told him about my earlier contacts on the edge of death with the two guides, and of the spaces that I had been in with LSD. I told him of my childhood history in the Catholic church and of the visionary experiences of my youth.

Oscar confirmed those parts of each of the experiences that I had felt were essential and real. They were real parts of me, realities that I had explored outside of myself but were apparently inside myself in what Sidney Cohen called "the beyond within." After I had given Oscar a detailed account of my cosmic computer experience (see Chapter 5), he said, "You have burned an immense amount of Karma* with that experience. That is the way to burn Karma for those who can do it without burning up their connection with Essence. You must have had help from other levels to have been able to go through that experience." Some esoteric schools use that technique with rare individuals, but they do not recommend its use in general.

---

* Burning Karma is making conscious the consequences of your past without shame, fear, anger or censoring.

I confirmed the fact that I had had help from other levels. I mentioned the two guides and the programming from Helen Bonnie to get to the two guides on that experience. I also saw, rather unequivocally, paths by which I could have flunked out in the cosmic computer experience. At any point, I could have shut out the experience, and not have stored it in memory because it was too painful. According to the esoteric tradition, this would have been very bad because one would have gone through the experience without the benefits of it, without the necessary negative reinforcement that it brought about in me.

In order to burn Karma, one must be wide awake, no matter what is happening to one. At no point during an either negative or a positive experience of a high energy level, can one afford to shut off one's consciousness. If one is going through a pure negative experience, the extreme negative emotion should be allowed to be imprinted on this negative space so that one's self-metaprogrammer does not return there. It is only the purest negative experiences that are worth recording to serve as guideposts to avoid this space entirely in the future. By means of pure experience set up in memory, as soon as this negative space starts to operate within one's self one can do the necessary things to shift to a positive or neutral space.

Thus, with Oscar, I saw that Karma burning, at least in part, consists of setting up in memory certain kinds of experiences with a powerful negative sign on them to prevent their reoccurrence. To state it rather simply, if one is going to stay in positive spaces, one must have an automatic avoidance program for the negative states built into the biocomputer. Once implanted, this enables the computer to operate on the positive side.

In a similar fashion, it is necessary during highly positive states to remember the experiences as positive and rewarding, so they will attract one automatically back to those spaces. This, too, is part of one's Karma in the sense that, without essential experiences in the highly positive spaces, one has great difficulty in knowing how to return there. If one has had experiences in the highly positive spaces, it is sufficiently rewarding so that one wishes to return there and one learns the routes.

There is an almost automatic reward system built into each of us in the sense that in the uterus, in childhood, we were in positive states continuously, though not necessarily consciously. We had to be brought out of the positive state in order to see where we were, and to realize that it was punishing to be removed from the positive and rewarding to return there. Kahlil Gibran said it as, "To know joy, one must know sorrow."

Oscar said that Karma was anything that brought us out of the positive places and continued to do so. Pure panic, pure horror, pure guilt could be experienced and thus serve as future avoidance points. With this kind of repeated training running through one's autobiographical material, one could eventually reach permanent positivity or Satori consciously in maturity without the automatic downers and without the automatic unconscious staying in the positive states without knowing where one was.

To be the Gurdjieffian man, the awake man, a higher level of man, is to stay awake in order to store positively and negatively reinforced experiences. To eventually stay in the higher states, to eventually integrate the higher states into one's ordinary life, is the goal of the awake man.

This way of looking at the work of spiritual development enabled me to finally decide to return to Chile and take the course. Oscar's empirical approach to spiritual development appealed to me since I, too, liked to do things empirically. Since Oscar did not ask me to believe things that I had not experienced myself, I was intrigued. As we discussed my role as an explorer of far-out spaces, an investigator, it developed that this empiricism was exactly the position I should take in the training.

I could start with any set of beliefs that I wished and I would probably have to get rid of some of them, if not all of them, as I progressed, but this would be up to me. Oscar said he was not trying to convince anybody except by direct personal experience of the phenomena. I found Oscar's program to be in line with what I wanted to do. In addition, I was impressed with him personally.

This approach fitted in with my own particular tendencies. As I stated in *Programming and Metaprogramming in the Human Biocomputer*, I am an explorer. If I try to exploit rather than to explore, I am prejudiced in my explorations. (Any exploiting tendency preprograms, any trips that I take, and it causes certain phenomena to occur again and again.) If one has repeating programs, below one's level of awareness, under these circumstances they tend to repeat and prevent one from finding new spaces.

Thus, in that one-week trip to Chile in May of 1970, I was able to see something of the framework of the training that Oscar was proposing to give. Even though I couldn't see the full panorama, I had glimpses into spaces that I wanted to go as well as spaces to which I had been and wished to return.

I had some doubts that I kept to myself. I did not like the idea of being in a closed group, esoteric or otherwise. I have pursued my own path, learning from whomever and wherever I could. In my experience, the politics inherent in many group decisions lower the quality and the effectiveness of the action. The experienced, wise, energetic, intelligent individual functioning in a loose coalition with others in a wide network is far more effective than he is in a tightly organized group, or so it seems to me.

Chapter 11
SECOND TRIP TO CHILE: STATES OF CONSCIOUSNESS DEFINED

On my second trip to Arica, I spent the first month at the Hosteria until about July 15, when I found a small, brand new house in a development near the University of the North (Universidad del Norte) on the Azapa Road.

Our first lessons began even before the first of July. Marcus Llana (Oscar's associate) came to teach the group the gymnastics exercises. The early-arrival group, Bob, Nancy, Steve, Linda, already knew these exercises. On the first of July we met for the first time in the local hospital in the nurse's lecture room. Oscar officially opened the training with a small ceremony and immediately got under way telling us what we were going to be doing. The early schedule consisted of physical exercises called the "Gym" for two hours a day, five to six days a week. We did auditions for an hour, chanting for another hour, mentations of various sorts for an hour or two and finally in the evening, group exercises with Marcus and Iris, another associate of Oscar. In the early days of the training, we met in the hospital for the lectures and met in an abandoned factory for the Gym, the group movement, and group chanting exercises.

On Sundays, we met in the desert at a location that Oscar had used previously and was continuing to use with the Chilean group. These exercises were called the "Pampas," a Spanish name meaning "the desert." It was a very vigorous set of exercises, which took anywhere from two to three hours depending on our physical condition. It involved walking certain courses in special ways, carrying rocks and praying.

Oscar defined his own particular concepts of the "Satoris."* His Satoris are defined as different positive levels (+24, +12, +6, +3) or states of consciousness. Oscar used the Gurdjieffian vibrational numbers[†] to specify the states of consciousness. In Table 1, we see these various positive and negative vibrational levels. The positive levels are +3, +6, +12 and +24. The neutral level is 48. The vibrational levels of 96, 192, 384 or 768 correspond to the (anti-Satori) states of. -24, -12, -6, and -3 respectively.

Almost everybody, sometime in their lives, experiences most of these states spontaneously. The memory of such experiences can be activated by developing a level 48 map. This is one path into these states. "Oh yes, I've been there before" is a common realization expressed in 48 on return from the other states. I wish to emphasize this point:

---

* Note on the use of the word "Satori": the classical traditional use of the Japanese term seems to confine its use to Oscar's "+3" and higher states. Oscar seems to use it for "lower" states for didactic purposes to give one steps of familiar experience in the positive direction. I found his formulation useful but I use another symbol (e.g. "+" state) for the four states of +3, +6, +12 and +24.

† For further analysis of the Gurdjieffian vibrational numbers, see: P. D. Ouspensky's The Fourth Way; New York, Knopf, 1957, and In Search of the Miraculous; New York, Harcourt Brace.

These states are definitely part of our human heritage, available to most of us.

In the lectures that Oscar gave us about these vibration levels and states of consciousness it became clearer to me that a lot of my previous experiences could be mapped using these concepts. For example, a large fraction of my life had been spent in 48 learning and teaching. A large fraction had been spent in 24 doing laboratory work, research on dolphins, writing, and similar activities. At times, while involved in these activities, I would slip into 96 (or -24) and continue to do the job in spite of the fact that it was no longer pleasant. My first trip on LSD was mainly in +12 although part of it, the episode in which I went to heaven with God on the throne seemed to be in +6.

While in coma, near death in 1964, I had been in +3 and +6. The episodes with the guides all took place in level +6. The hypnosis trip was +6. My +3 episode was the one in which I was taken out of the universe as we know it and was shown it speeded up a hundred billion times. I was shown it being created, expanding, and then falling back into a point – into the void. I was taken there by the creators and was shown to be one of the creators.

My migraine attacks were definitely at the level of -12. The pain was so great that I was constricted by the pain in great contrast to +12 where I was expanded by the love and energy. I found in the near-death experience of 1964, when I thought I was finished, that I had gone straight to -6 and then the two guides had brought me to the +6 level. I was in +6 and -6 under LSD in the tank experiences in the Virgin Islands. I, as a point, got into regions with vast entities, the "cognitional carnivores," as I called them at that time. At times

I was held for a very long time in a minus state, as in the -3 trip, "The Guided Tour of Hell" with Sandy Unger at the Spring Grove state hospital. Oscar's new maps allowed me to plot where I had been and enabled things to fall into place better so I could store them systematically and consider them in a new light.

Among our other school activities were the general sessions with Oscar in which he lectured and showed us mantra, chants, and so forth. We kept notes during these lectures. We also kept another notebook in which we maintained a journal of internal happenings within each one of us.

TABLE 1   *Levels of Consciousness*

Gurdjieff Vibration Level	States of Consciousness	Samadhi* Dharma-Megha Samadhi	Description
3	+3	Dharma-Megha Samadhi	Making the Ma'hdi. Classical Satori. Fusion with universal mind, union with God; being one of the creators of energy from the void, in the Ma'h spiritual center above the head.
6	+6	Sasmitanir bija	Making the Buddha. A point source of consciousness, energy, light, and love. Point of consciousness, astral travel, traveling clairaudience, traveling clairvoyance, fusion with other entities in time. In the Path mental enter in the head.
12	+12	Sananda	Blissful state, making the Christ, the green qutub, realization of Baraka, the reception of divine grace, cosmic love, cosmic energy, heightened bodily awareness, highest function of bodily and planetside consciousness, being in love, being in a positive LSD energy state. In the Oth emotional center in the chest.
24	+24	Vicara	The level of professional Satori or of basic Satori. All the needed programs are in the unconscious of the biocomputer, operating smoothly, the self is lost in pleasurable activities that one knows best and likes to do. In the Kath moving center in the lower belly.

Gurdjieff Vibration Level	States of Consciousness	Samadhi* Dharma-Megha Samadhi	Description
48	±48	Vitarka	The neutral biocomputer state, the state for the absorption and the transmission of new ideas; for the reception and transmission of new data and new programs; doing teaching and learning with maximum facilitation, neither in a positive or a negative state, neutral. On the earth.
96	-24†		Negative state; pain, guilt, fear, doing what one has to do but in a state of pain, guilt, fear; the state of slightly too much alcohol; of a small amount of opium; of the first stages of lack of sleep.
192	-12		Extremely negative body state where one is still in the body, as in an intense migraine attack, in which one's consciousness is shrunk down and inhibited and the awareness is only in the present in one's pain. The pain is such that one cannot work or do one's usual duties. A limitation is placed upon one's self, one is isolated, a bad inner state.
384	-6		Similar to +6 except that it is extremely negative. A purgatory like situation in which one is only a point source of consciousness and energy; fear, pain, guilt in the extreme; meaninglessness prominent.

Gurdjieff Vibration Level	States of Consciousness	Samadhi* Dharma-Megha Samadhi	Description
768	-3		Like +3 in that one is fused with other entities throughout the universe but these are all bad and one's self is bad and meaningless. This is the quintessence of evil, the deepest hell of which one can conceive. This can be an extremely high energy state lasting eternally, though by the planetside clock, one is there for only a few minutes. No hope in this state. No hope of escape from it. One is there forever. (See the Cosmic Computer write-up in the chapter entitled "The Guided Tour of Hell.")

---

* These are from *the Science of Yoga*, by t. K. Taimni. Wheaton, Ill.:Quest paperback, Theosophical Pub., 1967, pp. 38 and 61.

† Negative spaces have no real location; each is imagined as located in same region as corresponding positive space.

Oscar taught us about "ego deviations" and how he related them to the mentations and to our astrological rising sign as determined by our birth time and place. Astrologers have very simple tables for determining rising signs. If one has one's rising sign, one can then determine how one's mentations are deviated, that is, how one's ego is deviated and how one makes certain mistakes by confusing certain ideas with other ideas or certain kinds of happenings with other kinds of happenings. Every rising sign except Aries has ego-deviations associated with it.

During these lectures my disbeliefs about astrology in general were activated. For me the concept of the position of the constellations and the earth's position around the sun as primary determinants of personality and preprogramming forces on one's life course have always seemed irrelevant. Constellation position can be exactly determined but a person's variables can not be quantitated. I decided to temporarily accept Oscar's theory to try it and see what, if anything, was in it. His theory led me to look at certain ideas in a new way. This does not prove its "truth"; it shows only its didactic usefulness. Using these ideas I associated new connections between old events and removed certain blocks to moving into new states. Here I wish to state enough of Oscar's ideas so the reader can see how I moved where I did.

To determine the ego deviations associated with a non-Aries rising sign, find the mentation in Table 2 corresponding to one's rising sign. For example, Capricorn is my rising sign and it corresponds to charisma. Form a third column in the table by putting the mentation corresponding to one's rising sign opposite the substance mentation. For my particular case, since Capricorn is my rising sign, charisma is put opposite substance in the third column. Continue to form column 3 by listing in order the mentations given in column 2 following your rising sign mentation. When you get to the bottom of the column 2 list of mentations, start at the top of column 2 and continue until you again reach your rising sign mentation. Table 3 shows the completed column 3 for a Capricorn rising sign and Table 4 for any rising sign.

Now one assigns a certain width to the mentations that are in quotations. The width corresponds to the width of the astrological houses. There is a certain amount of overlap of the true mentations in column 2 and the deviated mentations in column 3. For example, "capacity" overlaps means and goals in my particular case. By my birth, on a particular time of day in a particular place, I had a "false" capacity for the true means and the true goals. (For those more deeply interested in such ideas, the exact data are 7:30 a.m., CST, January 6, 1915, St. Paul, Minnesota. I understand that one can work out the overlaps from these data plus the proper tables. Here I give only enough data for my own narrative purposes.)

TABLE 2

"True" Relationship Between Mentations and Rising Sign

SIGN	TRUE MENTATION
Aries	Substance
Taurus	Form
Gemini	Possibilities
Cancer	Needs
Leo	Impulse
Virgo	Assimilation
Libra	Elimination
Scorpio	Orientation
Sagittarius	Capacity
Capricorn	Charisma
Aquarius	Means
Pisces	Goals

TABLE 3

Deviated Mentations For Capricorn Rising Sign

SIGN	TRUE MENTATION	DEVIATED MENTATION
Aries	Substance	"Charisma"
Taurus	Form	"Means"
Gemini	Possibilities	"Goals"
Cancer	Needs	"Substance"
Leo	Impulse	"Form"
Virgo	Assimilation	"Possibilities"
Libra	Elimination	"Needs"
Scorpio	Orientation	"Impulse"
Sagittarius	Capacity	"Assimilation"
Capricorn	Charisma	"Elimination"
Aquarius	Means	"Orientation"
Pisces	Goals	"Capacity"

TABLE 4

Deviated Mentations in Terms of Various Rising Signs

DEVIATED MENTATIONS FOR RISING SIGNS

True Mentation (Aries)	Taurus	Gemini	Cancer	Leo	Virgo
Substance	Form	Possibilities	Needs	Impulse	Assimilation
Form	Possibilities	Needs	Impulse	Assimilation	Elimination
Possibilities	Needs	Impulse	Assimilation	Elimination	Orientation
Needs	Impulse	Assimilation	Elimination	Orientation	Capacity
Impulse	Assimilation	Elimination	Orientation	Capacity	Charisma
Assimilation	Elimination	Orientation	Capacity	Charisma	Means
Elimination	Orientation	Capacity	Charisma	Means	Goals
Orientation	Capacity	Charisma	Means	Goals	Substance
Capacity	Charisma	Means	Goals	Substance	Form
Charisma	Means	Goals	Substance	Form	Possibilities
Means	Goals	Substance	Form	Possibilities	Needs
Goals	Substance	Form	Possibilities	Needs	Impulse

Libra	Scorpio	Sagittarius	Capricorn	Aquarius	Pisces
Elimination	Orientation	Capacity	Charisma	Means	Goals
Orientation	Capacity	Charisma	Means	Goals	Substance
Capacity	Charisma	Means	Goals	Substance	Form
Charisma	Means	Goals	Substance	Form	Possibilities
Means	Goals	Substance	Form	Possibilities	Needs
Goals	Substance	Form	Possibilities	Needs	Impulse
Substance	Form	Possibilities	Needs	Impulse	Assimilation
Form	Possibilities	Needs	Impulse	Assimilation	Elimination
Possibilities	Needs	Impulse	Assimilation	Elimination	Orientation
Needs	Impulse	Assimilation	Elimination	Orientation	Capacity
Impulse	Assimilation	Elimination	Orientation	Capacity	Charisma
Assimilation	Elimination	Orientation	Capacity	Charisma	Means

Each one of the mentations is a totally independent variable. One's substance, for example, does not depend on anything but itself. It is truly unique and absolutely separate from all the other mentations. One's substance does not necessarily reflect one's form nor does one's form reflect one's substance. Substance, form, possibilities, needs, impulse, assimilation, elimination, orientation, capacity, charisma, means, and goals are all completely independent of each other. In a deviated case, however, one confuses some of these ideas with other ideas and puts in dependent relationships which do not exist.

In my particular case, my most important deviation (according to Oscar) was my confusion of my strength or capacity with my means and goals. He said that I constructed a false capacity, a false strength based upon the means and the goals that I chose. I felt that my strength depended upon setting my goals and setting my means. I had to choose my means in a certain way or else I would not have strength. This is, of course, nonsense. One has a certain strength independent of the means that one chooses or the goals that one has.

During the week in August, I saw how this pattern of confusion had influenced my choice of career, marriages, and so forth. I had previously worked on the confusion of each mentation with each other mentation. I had spent approximately a week working up a table and considering deeply this kind of confusion. I had dealt with the confusion of charisma for substance and of substance for charisma, my first deviated mentation. I tended to assume that a person's substance was reflected by their charismatic self which they were projecting to me. It was a particularly important mistake to me. When I detected a person's substance, I immediately felt they radiated this and that this was their charisma. I was caught up short when I found that certain people, whose substance I could see and feel, did not even know that they had an Essence or were not acquainted with their substance at all and did not realize that they were radiating the Essence. My confusion was double: finding a person with a powerful charisma, I mistook it for "substance"; detecting an Essence, I presumed the person was conscious of it when he wasn't, as if it were "charisma." I made this mistake many times. I finally realized what it was – confusion of charisma and substance. I put in a lot of work on these ideas. I also found that in the past, I had corrected several of the deviations.

Chapter 12
PHYSICAL BARRIERS TO POSITIVE STATES: PHYSICAL EXERCISES

Ida Rolf and Fritz Perls taught me that one can keep "tape loops" from earliest childhood going in one's body-muscle-brain circuits. Some of these tapes are fixated orders to stay out of good spaces. They are "ego fixations" or "downer" orders in one's biocomputer. One can clear some of these orders out by being Rolfed physically by someone like Ida and mentally by someone like Fritz. Beyond this clearing, one needs a responsive, highly energetic body for the higher positive status – hence, the exercises or "Gym" as we called it.

The first large barrier to positive states of +24, +12, +6 and +3 is one's physical condition. In order to overcome this first barrier, we had started at the beginning of the training to do the Gym. The changes in my body as a result of the Gym exercises and the Pampas exercises, together with the psychological changes I made, enabled me to reach +3 (classical Satori or dharma-megha Samadhi).

What is the Gym? It is a set of about three dozen physical exercises mainly based on Hatha Yoga and Aikido, which use every muscle, every joint of the body and which massage the internal organs and tone up the vestibular apparatus in the inner ear and reorient the whole bodybrain configuration.

A detailed description of these exercises does not serve my purposes here. It is sufficient for those persons interested to say that there are a half dozen Hatha Yoga positions (sphinx, cobra, shoulder stand, headstand, plow), some of Air Force exercises (leg lifts on back, scissors, bicycle, etc.), some modified yoga movements (similar to the-going-to-the-sun-group), and dance and ballet steps. There are no new movements or positions. Possibly a new aspect is the sequencing and timing. Music (such as Santana Abracsas) is an added element of rhythm and speed, which gives me pleasure. Done in the morning I find Gym an energy source.

I started with about two hours per day for the Gym; after a year I can do the whole sequence in 20 to 30 minutes. As I began the exercises, I went into some very bad places with them because my body was protesting the new movement and positions. In the beginning, the exercises themselves were a barrier to the positive states in the sense that I was left in a negative state as a result of the early practice of the exercises. However, as I achieved better physical condition, it became more and more likely that I would go on a high from the exercises. Eventually I got into states +24 and +12 doing the Gym.

Between each exercise, I meditate briefly in a relaxed position until the reverberations of sensation through the body have calmed down. I keep the mind as blank as possible.

Eventually the Gym seemed to do itself while I sat off at the side and watched as it took place in complete peace.

After approximately one month of this Gym, I went into my first state +12 and was able to do Gym during state +12. I then found out what some of these movements really were. Until one does the Gym and directly experiences in one's own body all of these movements and the general patterns that develop out of the individual movements and their relationship to one another, one cannot predict what will happen inside oneself. (See Chapter 15.)

There seems to be total reprogramming of the whole body and of the mind by going through these movements every day. The older one is, the more important it is that one does them every day. I found that the accumulation of stiffness by leaving out one day is almost too much. Younger people will not understand this statement, but the older people will.

One of the traps for the younger people is that the sheer joy of movements will carry them into an ecstasy that will lead them astray from the major part of the work. This may be a necessary trip for a particular youngster. It should be pointed out that this can happen and probably will happen with most younger people so they should be ready for this and continue in spite of this kind of seduction.

The rest of the physical program consisted of the Pampas exercises, which were done every Sunday morning. These exercises were designed to develop the whole body as a total functioning unit, including respiration, circulation, and general metabolism. With the general body stress of these experiences, I broke through the body's general negative states and death fears – some of my negative downer programs.

The group met in the pampas every Sunday and each person was given a particular schedule to follow for the six exercises. Each exercise included a mantram or a prayer to be coordinated with the movements of the body. Each exercise was done on a special course that had been marked out on the desert.

THE PAMPAS

The Ellipse Exercise

This exercise is done around the top of a hill. This is a conical hill with an elliptical course paced out around the sloping base. (The base of our hill went up approximately fifty feet and the top of the cone went up about seventy feet.) At the beginning of this exercise, as in all following exercises, I do an Om, folding the hands and bowing toward the top of the hill. I climb as rapidly as I can to the top of the cone and do the Opening Lotus exercise three times facing toward the sun. In the Opening Lotus, my hands are raised above the head, palms facing about a 45 degree angle toward the sun, eyes closed; my arms are then brought down over the chest, forearms together, backs of hands together, and the head bent down over the hands. At the same time that I do the Opening Lotus, I say, "From thee we come; to thee we go." Then I run down the hill and take the elliptical rising course around the hill. I do this course clockwise three times, once for each of the centers; once for the Kath, once for the Oth, once for the Path. A trip to the top of the hill is made between each of these elliptical tours. (The Kath center is located four fingers below the navel. The Oth center is located in the center of the chest. The Path center is at the hairline in the middle of the forehead.)

This was a very strenuous exercise. When I was in good condition, it would take about forty-five minutes. At the beginning, it took about an hour and one-half. I could make the course very rapidly if in good condition, but took it slowly if in poor condition. Some of my most moving experiences took place on the ellipse.

The Kath Hill Exercise

On the valley floor, I pick up a rock that I can recognize later. I face the Kath hill, which is about one hundred feet high and has a 45 degree angle slope, and salute with the rock. I project the Kath center up the hill, carry the rock up the hill in the right hand, and as I go up the hill, I imagine that the Kath is pulling me up. When I reach the top, I put my Kath center in the rock. I throw the rock with the Kath in it down the hill and then run down the hill after it; I find it and put the Kath center back into the body. This is a relatively short but vigorous exercise and trains one on the proper use of the Kath energy for total body movement. I found it an interesting "as if" program.

I Listen and I Obey Exercise

I salute the I Listen and I Obey course at the bottom and inhale while standing still. On the exhale, I take seven steps. I say one syllable on each step, dividing up "I Listen and I Obey" into seven syllables. After finishing the seven steps, I stop in place and meditate and listen. As the course gets less steep, I open my eyes. (There was a cliff at the edge of our hill, dropping a thousand meters to the pacific Ocean.) When I finish at the top, I run down or walk down freely.

(The men do this course once and the women do it three times. The reason that Oscar gave for the women doing it three times is that they have a much harder time listening.) This exercise is a relatively relaxing one and was welcome after the more vigorous ones.

The Shotput

I start with a salute on the valley-floor course. I pick up a large stone of five or ten pounds. I walk the course using the right arm for the shotput; I come back down using the left arm. The instant that I am projecting the stone at shoulder level. I release the air with a loud noise such as "Oh." I put all of my impulse out through the throat. I do one round trip. I must watch out for other people using the same course for the next two exercises in order not to hit them.

The Forced March

I start with a salute on the valley-floor course. I walk around the half-mile course three times. I coordinate the mantrum "Have Pity" with one step per syllable. I inhale on the three steps of "Have Pity." I hold my breath on the next three steps. I exhale on the next six steps, saying "Have Pity; Have Mercy." I do this exercise smartly swinging the arms in a definite fashion at a definite marching pace.

Dead Weight Exercise

This exercise is also done on the valley-floor course. I select and salute a very large stone that I can comfortably carry. I suspend the rock chest high six inches from the body on the palms. This rock is my Karma. As I make three round-trips, I coordinate the prayer, "All is Thine" I am allowed to shift the rock close into the chest when I become tired.

This exercise was rather wearing at the beginning. It gradually became easier and easier. I could always increase the difficulty of it by picking a larger, heavier rock.

The Pampas exercises were done at about a thousand meters above the Pacific Ocean about five miles from Arica.

The exercises started out the week with a bang every Sunday and gave a tremendous amount of energy, which was used during the week.

When I started the Pampas exercises in July, I felt that they were tearing me down and it wasn't until after four weekends of doing them that I suddenly realized, when I finally made state +12, why we were doing them. My body was in better shape than it had been in for ten years. Apparently top physical condition is necessary in order to make +12.

During the Pampas, I went through several "physical death-rebirth" experiences. I pushed myself into regions of exertion beyond what I thought were my limits. I literally risked what I conceived of as overexertion, with "heart-failure" as the expected result. This "heart-failure" did not occur. I found I had gone through a barrier of fear in the body and into a new high-energy space of physical functioning which was a prerequisite for me to achieve +12. To go up, I had to push through that which held me down – fear of bodily death – an unconscious component of the downer programs, or, in Oscar's terms, "body-ego" or body fixations of ego.

Chapter 13
STATE 48: THE HUMAN BIOCOMPUTER

In this and the following chapters on the different states of consciousness, I give my descriptions of the states as I know them, in my own language. Despite the frequent use of the third person and the passive mode of speech, this is me, the scientist-explorer, giving you his sketches of territory he has explored. In this mode I lay down the context, the background, for the accounts of my own experiences, which are given in the first person singular. In a sense, that which I give impersonally is metaprogramming for me in the past and metaprogramming for you in the present given in order that you may understand the personal descriptions.

For those interested in expanding their own awareness, this chapter and the ones on states +24, +12, +6, and +3, I consider as basic steps. Each statement or idea or metaprogram expressed is derived from deep personal experience and many hours of concentration, contemplation, meditation, and thought.

In conversations with Oscar Ichazo, I introduced to him the contents of my monograph, *Programming and Metaprogramming in the Human Biocomputer.* He read the monograph and we discussed it at length. As a result of these conversations, I define vibration level 48 as that state of consciousness in which one is operating his human biocomputer completely rationally, without either positive or negative emotion. The emotions are in a neutral state, yet the energy can be high. At this level of consciousness, one is absorbing data, programs, or metaprograms. One is inserting new metaprograms or ideas into the storage banks of one's biocomputer. One can also be in 48 while giving new ideas to another person. One of the ways of testing if you are in 48 is to observe your interaction with another person. If there is relatively no emotion present, either in a positive pleasure sense or in a negative sense, then one may be at level 48, whatever its quality.

Sometimes it is difficult to know whether those parts of the biocomputer outside of one's level of awareness are really operating in 48. If one is in the grips of some ego program and identifying with it, the ego can be shouting, "I am in level 48!" whereas one really is in some other level, 96 or lower. To really be in any level, from 48 to +3, one must be in truth at that level and not pretending that one is at that level. A clean 48 has very little of such garbage left in it.

With separate control systems operating in a separated, disassociated or fragmented state within a given human biocomputer, parts of the biocomputer can be at different levels. One control center may be at 192, another at 96, another at 48. The self-metaprogrammer may be moving around among these three control systems or it may be simultaneously identified with each of them. In this state, the human biocomputer has not yet reached the degree of unity required to name its own state in a pure, unitized fashion.

To be in a pure 48 (neutral energy) requires the unification and integration of separate control centers so that at least a majority of the operational machinery of a given biocomputer is subsumed under the one central self-metaprogrammer. To reach this unity, the body and the mind must be in top shape and the spiritual path well defined and accepted. If one knows what is meant by "top physical condition" then that is one's physical goal. If one doesn't know by personal experience what "top physical condition" is, one can't know what a pure high energy 48 is. In such a case, one will have to do physical exercises of the individual body-part type such as the Ichazo Training "Gym" or Hatha Yoga in addition to total body stress exercises such as the "Pampas" exercises or severe jogging. If one has to learn what "top physical condition" is, one has a longer, harder road than those who have already experienced this beneficent state of the body. Why is this state necessary to achieve a unitized level of 48?

Poor physical shape means that we have not been getting sufficient exercise every day to keep the biocomputer in a controllable, quiescent, bland state at high-energy level. In poor physical shape, there are impulses not under one's control that make one restless. One moves about and does aimless kinds of actions with unknown desires taking the stage at awkward times.

There can be a lot of mental noise going on in one's head; one can talk practically incessantly to oneself and to other people in one's head. As one gets into good physical shape, this kind of impulsive internal and external activity tends to lessen considerably. One's 48 becomes more integrated, more unitized, and more of one's available biocomputer is utilized. In general, disciplined physical exercises tend to unitize the computations, the programming, the impulses of the biocomputer. One becomes more whole. One becomes more one's own self and functions less at the behest of unknowns in oneself and of other persons on the outside. Within a few days after starting a series of disciplined exercises, done daily, one can begin to see the results of this increased, almost unconscious, control, over one's biocomputer. The self-metaprogrammer assumes control over more of one's biocomputer. The paradox here seems to be that one subjects oneself to a regime or a program of exercises in order to achieve freedom from the noise inside one's own body and head. In Chile I found my inner impulsive noises decreasing as my physical condition improved.

As one's 48 improves with physical exercise, so one must do other kinds of exercises to further improve one's biocomputer and its functioning at level +8. Vibration levels 96 and lower are states of divisive action not under control of oneself. In these levels something inside of one is fighting against the obvious laws of one's own nature and the nature of the universe. One is doing or is exposed to those things that divide one from one's Essence. One's Essence is the highest expression of universal law as applied to humans, persons, bodies, and biocomputers.

To clean up one's biocomputer to the point where one's 48 is a unitized thing with a single, well-organized direction, one must do mental exercises as well as the physical. There are literally thousands of such mental exercises. Some are given in Jnana Yoga, some are given in the writings of Gurdjieff and his followers such as Ouspensky and Orage. Some are subsumed under such titles as "Christian Prayer," though one could argue that these are spiritual exercises more than mental or intellectual ones. I have given some of the mental exercises that I have found most useful in my book,

Programming and Metaprogramming in the Human Biocomputer and also in my workshops. Other helpful mental exercises, derived from Oscar Ichazo's teachings, are the mentations and the ego deviations of the mentations.

I repeat here a revised Table 5 from *The Human Biocomputer* showing the different stages of biocomputer functioning. This table itself is an intellectual exercise that can free one by mapping what one is in terms of modern science and modern scientific theory.

In this formulation, I place the unknown at the top. This epitomizes my position as an explorer. Beyond me, beyond us, beyond our current understanding, is the unknown. The unknown exists inside of us, outside of us, and among all our ideas having to do with all of this; therefore throughout the human biocomputer and its operations, the unknown is paramount.

TABLE 5

Schema of the Human Biocomputer

Levels of Structure

10 The Unknown

9   The Essence Metaprogramming

8   The Self-Metaprogramming

7   The Ego Metaprogramming

6   Metaprogramming in general
    (without reference to control system)

5   Programming

4   Brain's actions

3   The Brain as a physical structure

2   The Body as a physical structure

1   The External Reality in all of its aspects
    (including the body and the brain)

Today, I would estimate that we understand less than one tenth of 1 percent of what is going on in our body, in our brain or in our mind, and in our spirit. At any given instant a given human being can understand one thousandth of the realities inherent within himself, his external reality, and other humans. As distance from his conscious center increases, he knows less and less in a fast asymptotic, logarithmic decline of knowledge. The statement about the increase of ignorance with distance of course does not pertain if one can tune in on cosmic networks and become part of those networks in a conscious, functioning way. Understanding is limited; knowledge is still limited; but consciousness can be expanded beyond where it normally is in the consensus external and internal realities as dictated by our culture.

The Essence metaprogramming is that which leads to the highest positive states of consciousness and of Satori explained elsewhere in this book. In the human biocomputer, when one is in level 48, there are the ideas connected with the Essence that the self generates, that the self knows from previous experience, that the self feels with certitude are an absolute, objective reality. In a given biocomputer, this level of metaprogramming may be very weak or lacking.

One idea I have found useful is that one can increase the strength of the Essence metaprogramming in a given biocomputer by pragmatic, empirical technical experiences of the positive levels. Then that particular biocomputer can move more and more into the states of Essence and Essence metaprogramming. Eventually, a given biocomputer can, through the efforts of the self-metaprogramming level, construct and achieve states of the highest levels and thus move into the Essence, identifying with Essence itself — its metaprogramming. However, until a given self-metaprogrammer, a given biocomputer, has achieved the storage of essential metaprogramming, it cannot move into Essence metaprogramming levels. The first few jumps into Essence metaprogramming, the first few experiences of states of high positivity, if done consciously and if sufficiently modeled and stored within the biocomputer, then offer a pathway back to Essence metaprogramming.

The self-metaprogramming level of structure and of vibrational level 48 is where I am while writing for you, and is where you are while reading what I write. (See Table 6.) Level 48 is characteristic of the self-metaprogrammer in the best states. This is where one functions as a neutral agent, a fair witness of the mental processes, reorganizing them, taking in new information, giving out new information. As the levels of positive states begin to encroach on the self-metaprogrammer and one becomes more and more like and of Essence, the self-metaprogrammer disappears.

At structural level 9, Essence metaprogramming, one has the vibrational levels of the states +3, +6, +12 and +24. There is only a small fraction of Essence in 24. There is a full fraction of essence, say 99 percent Essence, in state 3. Therefore on structural level 9 we can consider the states of the biocomputer, the conscious states of the self, to be closer and closer to that of Essence in a quantitative way: 99 percent Essence at +3; 75 percent at +6; 25 percent at +12; 5 percent at +24, and 1 percent at 48. In a way, however, this is a transitional state of a given human biocomputer. These small fractions are the initial states as one begins to go toward Essence.

As the self-metaprogrammer decides the course it is going to take and begins to develop the Essence metaprogramming level, it begins to assume the metaprograms, "I am moving towards Essence; I am designing my life to see the true reality of Essence; I am going to do whatever is necessary to move into Essence." As this takes place, the positive states develop, the self-metaprogrammer moves into the Essence metaprogrammer and the whole question of time spent, schedules per week, and the like, becomes the question of how much of one's eternal present will one be in true Essence. This is a pragmatic, practical problem depending upon the planetside trip; it can't be decided in 48. It is put into the biocomputer as a super-self-metaprogram at structural level 8.

Structural level 7, the ego metaprograms, are the negative, below 48 vibrational levels: -24, -12, -6, and -3. The ego level is the level at which one has the conception that one is a powerful, independent entity and does not need the network, does not need the Essence, does not need any idea of the creators, does not need the mystical states. The list is endless but here is a sampling of ego programs (my own): "I end with the death of my body. I originated from the happenstance of the right molecules being in the right part of the universe at the right time. There are no creators; there is no guiding principle; there is no law forming us. There is no Essence, there is only the thermal dance, the ultimate thermodynamic death of the universe with the slow increase of entropy. There is no recycling of the universe; eventually it will run down. There is no life after death; there is no eternal life for any portion of our consciousness. There is no explanation for our origins, or those of the universe. We are a purposeless accident."

You can add to these from your own list. Anything that brings you down and out of vibration levels +48, +24, +12, +6, and +3 is an ego program. Any negative independent control system over and above yourself is an ego metaprogram.

There is a common paradox in understanding this ego as opposed to oneself. This is ego both in the sense of "downer programs" and in the sense of the knowledge and feeling that one is an independent, willful, desiring, powerful entity who is using the cosmic law and energy in the service of one's own "power trip." Cosmic energy and cosmic love are absolutely impartial, beyond choice. They can be employed by an individual (such as Hitler). However, once they are so used, the negative consequences to that particular ego can be rather overwhelming. Living in the law, living in the flow, going with it, allowing, giving up the initiative to the Satori levels, to

TABLE 6

Quantitative Relations between Self, Essence, and Ego Metaprograms
(Note: Self is mobile, Essence and Ego are Fixed)

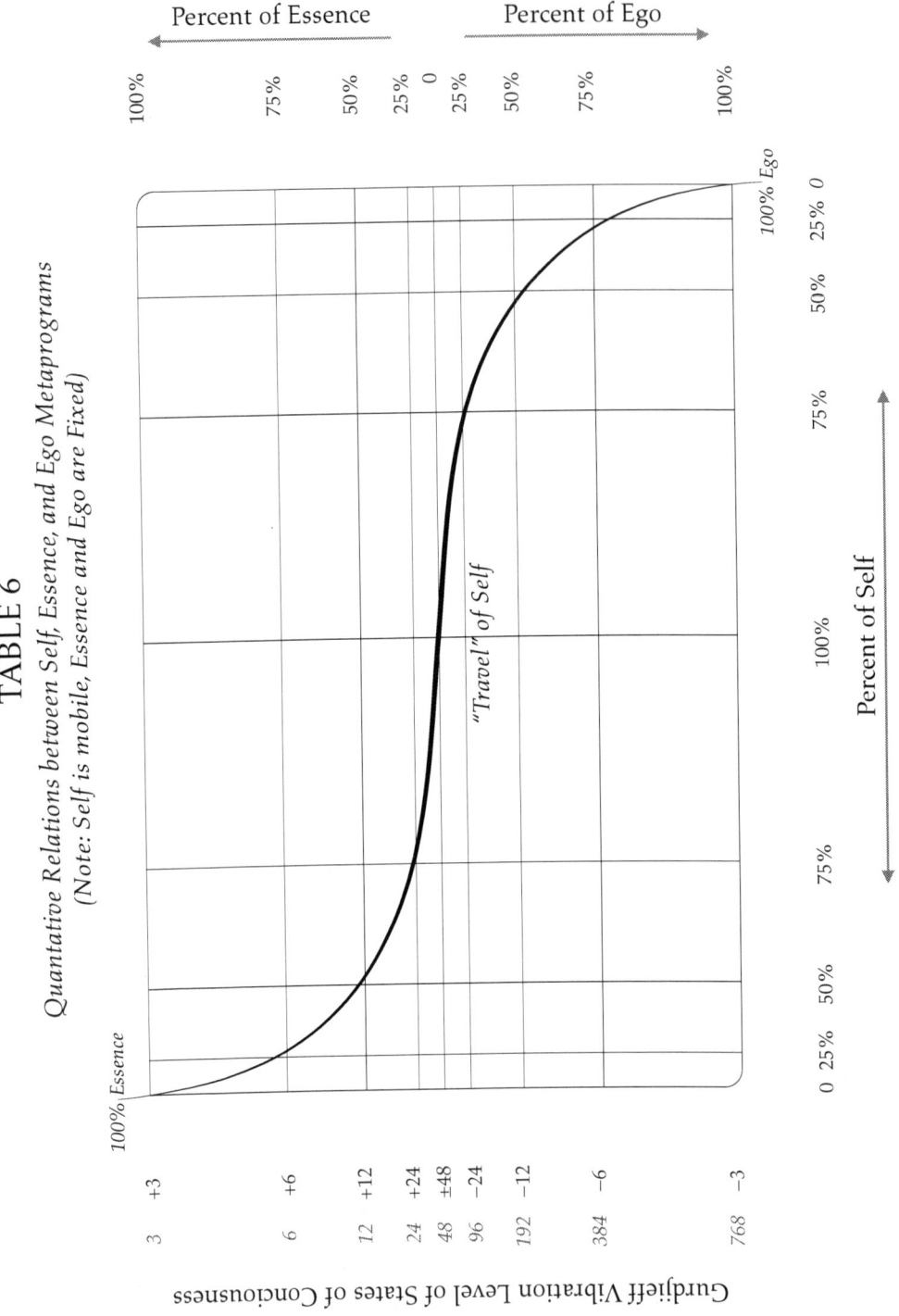

the Essence, to the network of Essences in the universe is the only antidote to an accumulation of Karma (for those who believe in Karma) that can destroy one again, again, and again, throughout eternity. As long as one holds onto the beliefs in the ego, as opposed to the beliefs in the Essence, one is in the service of self-destruction; one is under the dominance of phobic forces, of the true paranoia of being persecuted and prosecuted by the cosmic forces.

The three hours I spent on a -3 showed me unequivocally, by the extremely negative reinforcement, that I never again wanted to go back to the beliefs in -3 and to functioning at that level. The terror, the panic, the pain at that level are so extreme that my self-metaprogrammer will never again self-impose that level on this particular human biocomputer. In contrast, the rewards of +3 and a giving in to the flow at +3 are so great that I am drawn in that direction inescapably. The force pushing me away from -3 and the force pulling me toward +3 are large forces. This, then, is the beginning of Essence metaprogramming in my human biocomputer. The repulsion of -3 and the attraction for +3 leads finally to identification of the self-metaprogrammer with the Essence.

The fear of death is at -3; the joy of eternal life is +3; the dichotomies expressed here are characteristic of the self-metaprogrammer. In Essence there is no such dichotomy. One can see -3, +3 as identical. The only difference is in the attitude of the self-metaprogrammer, carried over into the Essence levels of functioning. Apparently, the uncontaminated pure Essence has no such dichotomies. Cosmic love does not take sides: it teaches through its agents, unequivocally, eternally, irreversibly.

In this chapter on level 48, I am functioning on level 48 as I give you the basic ideas for all of the other levels. Explanatory teaching is a basic function of level 48. By showing the maps with both ends of the spectrum of possible states, and by showing the control systems that I have experienced in my own human biocomputer, I hope to help you to analyze the functioning of your own biocomputer. Your human biocomputer may have to take these ideas and others and carry out a 48 integration for you in your own language. If you do not have the language that I have been using, I would advise you to read *Programming and Metaprogramming in the Human Biocomputer* and other books that can give you the necessary concepts to set up this metamodel.

My human biocomputer says there is a route toward Satori that is a head trip, that is an intellectual pathway, that is the Jnana Yoga route, the way of understanding in contrast to: the way of love, Bakti Yoga; the way of action, Karma Yoga; the way of energy, Tantra Yoga; the way of meditation; the Zen path; and so on. The level 48 path is to clean up one's human biocomputer and the levels above and below to where one has a clear point of view and a clear set of assumptions with which to work. One can then begin to reduce the power of the ego metaprogramming, to increase the power of the self-metaprogramming and to move toward the Essence metaprogramming.

Thus, in 48, I, my self-metaprogrammer, speaks to you, your self-metaprogrammer, giving you something of my general metaprogramming, which is this whole book, this whole approach, in order to move my self-metaprogrammer and your self-metaprogrammer into positive states at levels above 48. Writing this book, describing these to you, brings me into state +24, the basic professional state.

Chapter 14
STATE +24: THE BASIC PROFESSIONAL STATE

State +24, which corresponds to the vibrational level 24 state of consciousness, is called the basic positive state. I call it the "professional" state because here one needs no new information; one needs only to practice one's profession. Under profession I include all human activities that a person knows very well in his own right and that he can do without creating new metaprograms, programs or ideas.

Level 48 is the level for creative thought. It is the level to which we return from the higher levels in order to integrate the experiences of the higher levels. We integrate, map, and store at level +8. On level +24 we practice; we do that which we do best. No new programs are needed: we lose our self in practice. In our culture, this can happen in any profession. When an accountant is doing his figures that he knows so well, when a bookkeeper is working on his books, when anyone is enjoying the working process and no longer has an ego or even a self, when he is functioning totally within the framework of his enjoyment of his profession, then he is in state +24. A cabinetmaker doing his joinery, an artist painting a picture, a businessman in his conference room, a surgeon in the operating room, an engineer designing and building, a politician organizing legislation, the President meeting with his cabinet, military men working in the Pentagon, should all be examples of state +24.

The important part about +24 is the enjoyment and the automatic nature of what one is doing plus the loss of self, selfhood, and the absence of ego metaprogramming. In +24 one has turned control of the biocomputer over to the task in hand whatever this may mean in terms of the reality of body, mind, and spirit.

The golf professional in a tournament turns himself over to playing the game at each drive, at each stroke, at each putt. He grounds himself in his Kath and pushes the ball with whatever power is needed to accomplish a straightline flight toward the hole. He himself is lost in the process of body and mind coordination to deliver that ball to the correct place at the correct time with the correct velocity to prevent overshoot or undershoot. He may preprogram the game taking in full knowledge of a particular golf course, his competition, the crowd, and all the other variables that are entering into this competition. He preprograms in 48. Before going into level +24, he makes his plans, he modifies the program as necessary to accomplish the job and then enters the game in +24, no longer being creative unless it is absolutely necessary in case of an emergency during the game.

A champion skier in competition does a similar job. In his particular case, he must learn a given new race course in detail in 48, programming it into his biocomputer very carefully before he starts down the course in competition. 48 is then the preprogramming of the race course: looking at the snow conditions; looking at possible obstacles, such as where the crowd may be coming in on the course, where the snow fences are, where the holes are that haven't been filled, where the dangerous changes in slope are, where he may have to jump and lose contact with the ground, where he will have to turn at high speed; deciding how much speed will be needed. The program is already laid down in his biocomputer before he starts down from the top of the mountain, so that quite automatically in +24 later he will do the right thing. He will keep himself, as it were, in his Kath (his center of gravity) about one hundred yards ahead of where his skis are on the course. He will stay in +24 all the way down the mountain. Any instant he goes into 48 he is in tremendous danger; he may kill himself against a tree, against rocks, or with a very bad fall. The faster he goes, the higher the necessity of his remaining in +24. If he has the slightest doubt about his ability, any ego program that shows up to bring him out of +24 is incredibly dangerous. It is in such pursuits such as racing down a mountain on skis, racing a highspeed car or an ice boat, or racing a fast horse on a hunt course over walls and ditches that one must remain completely and utterly in +24 as a professional in order to avoid injurious or lethal "accidents."

The ego programs are inhibited, suppressed, put aside by the professional while he is doing his particular job. The more dangerous the job, the greater the necessity that he put aside the ego programs, that he take himself out of the picture and allow the automatic programming to take place. He must have confidence in the automatic performance required of him under these particular external reality conditions. One gives oneself up to the programming and does not misuse either the self-metaprogrammer or the ego programs. One stays more toward the side of one's own Essence.

Yet, one must not go out of state +24 into the more positive state +12 under these conditions. If one does, it is quite as dangerous as if one dropped to 48 or 96. Going into ecstasy or into a state of "cosmic love spreading to others" is not the thing to do while one is going fifty or sixty miles an hour down a mountain on a pair of skis, driving a high-speed car on a difficult course with a wet track, making one's first drive in a professional golf tournament, or coming up to the starting line in an ice boat race where one is about to go seventy miles an hour.

Here the danger is quite the opposite of going into ego programs. Here one would lose too much of the external reality programming by going into +12. In +12, the set of dimensions being enjoyed are different from those required by the planetside trip. State +12 should be kept for specific, can-be-controlled conditions where that is the appropriate thing to be done and where there is minimum danger to one's physical being doing it. Knowledge of a higher positive state helps one to understand the Satori levels beneath that level.

In contrast to +24, we have level 96 or -24. I refer you to the table of states of consciousness in Chapter 11. In level 96, one is forced to do that which one knows well, but some condition in oneself makes it a very negative performance. Instead of its being rewarding, as it is in +24, it is punishing. Instead of the positive reinforcement of the reduction of ego, one is in ego with a vengeance.

One can be on a bum trip with alcohol, barbiturates, heroin, morphine, or just on a bummer on a bad trip created by any means. However, one is still capable of functioning, must work, and must do the job that one knows how to do. Despite one's self, negative emotion, negative motivation, negative reinforcement, a bad trip takes over. One is still on the planetside trip. There are the requirements of that trip; one must keep one's body going under dangerous conditions. One must accept the bad trip, the negative reinforcement, to avoid sinking further down the scale of the states, the lowest vibrational levels. One is acutely aware of one's ego and the fact that one can't do anything about it. It seems as if one is going to be at level 96 or -24 forever. It is as if one cannot operate in such a way to move the metaprograms so that one can get to 48, the neutral level.

Part of the eternal present in -24 is generated by the fact that one really is not willing to leave 96 or -24. One may not know the map back because one has defined oneself as ignorant in this state. There can be a control system exerted by the ego for -24 which says, in effect, to the self-metaprogrammer, "Thou shalt not move from this state; thou shalt only get worse; thou shalt not get better."

In certain aspects of the Judaic, Christian, Catholic, and especially in the Calvinist traditions, man is born to 96 and hence it is the natural state, the state of the eternally damned, eternally avoiding the hell just below.

The natural, simple, easy, obvious and continuous state from childhood on is to be in the positive states. They are level +24 and above. What must be developed is a good 48. Minus 24 or 96 is only of use to teach what is below 48 and to learn enough about the negative states below 48 so that in 48 one has a good map of them and knows that the prime directive is not to go to those negative states but to stay at 48 or higher positive states.

Chapter 15
STATE +12: THE BLISSFUL SHARING BODY

A perspective of the State +12 level in relationship to other states can be gained by reviewing the Table of states (Table 1). One is in the body in "+12," but not doing a job on the planetside trip. The hallmark of "+12" is the cosmic love, baraka, divine grace, cosmic energy, that one feels. One is functioning as an agent, a valve, a channel for this special exciting delightful energy, bliss, ananda.

I will illustrate "+12" by my account of the parts of it that I have been privileged to explore. My account is taken from my personal notes and from a tape transcription of a conversation with Oscar. The episodes described here are quite different from those I'd experienced with LSD. Here, my consciousness is very much broader and less "driven." The first episode happened after I had broken through several major barriers: my physical fears and physical condition, my study of the complex relations between the mentations and my past history and problems.

During the first five weeks of the training, I had great physical difficulty. I was fifty-five years old and had not had much physical exercise for many months previous. I was living at the small hotel and it was very cold there in the middle of winter so there was no way of recovering when returning to my room from the exposure to the new physical exertion. I moved lower and lower and finally contracted a virus infection and was forced to go to bed for several days.

On July 15, I was able to move into a little house in a housing development, and things went better. In the next few weeks I was able to recover lost ground and to get into a far better state. Meanwhile, my dyadic partner and I had been doing a "see-saw" operation. When I would go up, she would go down; when she would go up, I would go down. Somehow we had developed an unconscious dyadic program – very unsatisfying to both of us. At one time I became so low over the situation with her that I asked Oscar's help. He scheduled a meeting with her for Tuesday at 11 a.m. I hit bottom on Monday night and thought I was never going to get up again.

After she left the house on Tuesday morning, I started analyzing ego deviations. Oscar had said I still had a bit left of the means and goals confusion with a false capacity and this was the one I was analyzing. Finally, after half an hour, I found the solution to my main confusion of ideas in this area. I had been trying by certain techniques – certain means – and by setting certain goals to increase my strength or my capacity. I had confused the spiritual trip with the means of the spiritual trip and had gotten my own capacity mixed up with this. In reality, the means of the spiritual trip, the goals of the spiritual trip and my own strength and ability to move into new states and spaces were quite independent variables.

Suddenly I saw this, understood it deeply, and started up, moving into a special state of consciousness that I had also experienced under LSD in the Virgin Islands. I entered state "+12."

It was as if a switch had been turned on somewhere inside me that put me into a new space. There was this step-change, sudden and abrupt – moving into the new space. Everything became sparkling, reverberating, and delightful. I wanted to bring other people to this beautiful, blissful state. I saw scintillating things in the air like champagne bubbles. The dirt on the floor looked like gold dust, a bird singing became a voice moving out through the cosmos and reflecting off the galactic center. My own voice, saying "Om," did likewise.

Everything became transparent. I saw cosmic energy moving into my body, being sent to others from all over my body. I saw my own aura; I saw the aura of others. I felt perfect; nothing was wrong with me or the earth or its peoples. Everything was perfect; all things were alive; all persons were precious and delightful. As the hours passed I traveled in a taxi across town to join the group for exercises together.

I went into the "happy idiot country." I grinned and cried with joy. Nancy, one of the group, and I had a delightful all-nonsense kind of exchange. I ate an apple – very, very slowly, with extreme relish, feeling the energy of the apple being transformed inside me into energy for my use and for the use of others. The apple was "stored cosmic energy" for me and other persons. I suddenly had a tremendous compassion for all of the people in the group, all the people in the world and moved into new areas of appreciation of my species.

After nine hours of bliss, during the movement session, I suddenly came out of this state. Immediately I went into a grief state since I could no longer be in that beautiful place. Thursday, August 5, I again returned to +12 for four hours.

It wasn't possible to meet with Oscar until a week later to talk over what had happened. The transcription of the tape from the conference (August 11, 1970) between Oscar and me on the first two Satori 12* episodes (August 3 and August 5) follows:

O   Now, John, at your orders.

J   Last Tuesday, a week ago, I spent nine hours in what I think is Satori 12. I don't know what 12 is. I know it was higher than 24 and I could kind of go between 24 and 12. But then I started to go even higher than that (than 12) I got very cautious. Suddenly somebody inside me told me that I wasn't ready to go there yet, that I'm not prepared enough to go to the next stage, 6 – even though I've been there before.

O   Yes, you have.

J   In the tank with LSD. I've been to Satori 6 – I think you call it 6.

O   Yes.

J   It's where the universe, what I call the roar of the cosmic motor, takes me over and I'm gone; I'm finished.

---

*See note, page 172 on the use of "Satori" term by Oscar.

O   Yes.

J   So, I almost went there Tuesday. I got to the edge of it and said, "No, not yet," and stayed where I was. I was in this state of extreme joy-fantastic delight.

O   That's 12.

J   In everything.

O   Yes, that's 12.

J   My body was transparent. Energies were coming in everywhere along the body. There was a flow of energy up and down, out the top, out the bottom, in and out at the sides.

O   That's 12 alright.

J   And I was just luminous and there were gold sparkles on everything: the dirt on the ground in the air. Then I came down when I got cold that night during movement class. I didn't want to come down. I didn't want to come back. Nine hours wasn't enough. I wanted to stay there so I was incredibly disappointed and grief-stricken – and tired.

O   Coming down?

J   Coming out of it. I didn't want to.

O   You came down to 24; you didn't go to 48. At this very moment, you are in a complete state of 24 here.

J   Yes, but compared to 12, 24 isn't where I want to be (I give a grievous laugh).

O   Yes, yes, same comparison as 24 and other states.

J   48.

O   Yes, 48. Not to be in the higher state and to be and to see the higher state is to be in disappointment.

J   I became very impatient to get back there. But why I'm impatient (and this may be my own deviation), I'm impatient because others won't come up with me – won't move from the lower levels – won't come with me. I'm impatient because my dyadic partner won't move – won't get in where she belongs – won't get into 24 and stay there. She keeps dropping to 48 and sometimes 96. I get so impatient and I don't like that in me. That's ego, you know.

O   No, it's not, because I don't agree with you on that point. On the contrary, it is your incredible love of the state that causes you to want everybody there.

J   Yes.

O   The state is like that. Not selfish. On the contrary, it is forgiving. You want everyone to share it.

J   On Thursday I went back (to 12) for four hours – at the exercise class-during audition, during chanting. This time it was the whole group and I was tuned into everybody. Everybody was

J   me; I was everybody. When we sang Rama Krishna, I was Krishna, I was Rama; they were me – on and on.

O   Yes, yes.

J   Identity with everyone everywhere and then I tuned in on my partner – brought her up. I could feel me bringing her up to 12.

O   Yes, yes, but yes.

J   And then Marcus. Marcus went way up and then I started to cry with joy, with relief – that I was there again. I was out in the other big part of the factory. Marcus was there. He was crying and we both met in 12 and that was incredible. To see someone else there in 12 too. It's so marvelous. You know, and to know right straight across from one face to face between the two of you. I just want to cry now thinking how magnificent it is.

O   Yes, it is. Now the thing is this, John. We are going to repeat the state more and more. You can do it. But we must do it together. So, because the thing is this. In this very moment in our group there are only three persons who can do it. You, Marcus, and me. We are the only three who can do it, but we are three now.

J   But I haven't done it very often. I've done it only twice – nine hours and four hours.

O   But you've done it.

J   That is right. First experiment is always the successful one.

O   You have the first. You are going to have all the time in the states you want. We have to proceed like this. You have to be a little bit patient with the other ones. (Don't try to hurry them up too much.) They are really in the fastest speed possible. I can't give more pressure there, I know I can't. Many of them can break; many, many of them can break. I can say that perhaps there is more than 30 percent that can break.

J   I can see that.

O   There is 70 percent that is already very well. Not for Satori 12, no, no. Things are not like that. But for 24, yes. You see, after the shock [he is referring to the special "shock" days of the week – Tuesday and Thursday] always everybody is more-or-less in 24 or for a little period they are. I'm not saying that because I do not want to say.

J   They can really be there in 12.

O   Very much so, all the time and then we are going to prove the state. Prove the position. This is another work – proving the state. Take them to 24, 24, 24. After that the work is going to be how to take them out from 24 and down. So, yes, they make the muscle for staying.

J   One has to know both directions – in and out.

O   Yes. The first direction – to get inside. The other – to move out.

J   In spite of wanting to stay there.

O   Yes, but with telling them all of the techniques of being in 24 all the time. But the first thing is the deviation. After the ego deviations, our next training is going to be this work. Next, we are going to work on how to make it 24 all the time.

J   Is that protoanalysis – or is that deviations?

O   No, deviations, deviations. With all the protoanalysis, we are ready for going into 12. [Protoanalysis is the assignment of one's ego to one of nine ego types.]

J   OK.

O   Completely 12. For you, you were doing it before the protoanalysis. That means that you are resolved. For you, it is going to something – for seeing there. Nothing else.

J   But I want it pinned down; I want it conscious.

O   Yes.

J   In your terms that seems to be much more succinct and concrete a way of expressing it than I've come across before.

O   It's better if you want to teach it, to learn it first so that you can teach it. Because it is the method to be taught. It's exactly the same method you've employed in your life. There can't be another one for you. But this one is step-by-step – very precise; step-by-step. That's the only difference. John, I told you that. Here you are going to find it exactly as you have already. But this time, you will learn how you can show it to another one.

J   For me, that's the important thing – the fact that it's teachable. You can teach the method; otherwise, it isn't worth anything. Sri Aurabindo, Ramakrishna, and all those other people couldn't really teach the method.

O   They couldn't. They could go there but they couldn't teach it. They were saying all the time how they were doing it. But each was only his own case. Yes, each his own case. A very special own case. And for having that special own case, you have to have his life – or in your case, have your life. It's impossible for someone else (to copy your way). You can be near to that more-or-less, but the exact case is impossible. You can't repeat it. That is one point that is very important, John. When you get in that state of 12, you need to give. Completely. You need to give. Completely needed.

J   I know.

O   Because you know somehow that in giving you are going to have more. That's true too. Because it's a thing that's got to work. It's like having a muscle that you have to keep training all the time for getting more alive.

J   I think that's what brought on the state. What put me in the 12 on Tuesday was my concern for my partner. Wanting her to move. Sunday, at the Pampas she was in a very bad state. She came back, she was ready to die; she was giving up. Monday, she was really far out; she was in a bad space. Then I came to you in tears and told you and asked you to see her and you agreed. There was this tremendous relief that you would see her – that you would share this.

O   Yes, Yes.

J   And that I could share this with you. Then the next morning when I woke up – within a half hour of waking up I could feel my deviation – the last one – confusion with capacity for means and goals. There it was. My partner with me right in it. Before she came over here to see you, I didn't know what it was. I was in a very high place and then while she was here with you I went higher and higher. Then the roar started and I pulled back, but I was riding on sharing with her; sharing with everyone; bringing everyone up. But especially her from her very low place.

O   She came from a really, really low. She went shweee, bump. But you could see from her face how much she had changed. It was incredible. Nevertheless she has these kinds of states as you can see. Suddenly she becomes completely purified; but in the next second she starts thinking and comes down immediately.

J   Right. She can center and be right there and I feel she is going into 24 approaching 12 and then bing, she is out of it. Out of 24 and 12. It's just like that; she may be there in 24 for ten minutes, or five minutes, or something like this.

O   In the beginning it's like that.

J   Then why did I go nine hours?

O   That is you. You are not the proper training measure in this group, John.

J   Most people do it this way? Most people do it the way she's doing it?

O   Yes.

J   Micro-Satori? [short episodes.]

O   Everybody has micro-Satori; not all the time.

J   I was talking to Steve Stroud and he said five minutes is the most he's had.

O   Yes, Steve. Linda too, has the same, perhaps for a little longer because of her space – her pregnancy.

J   What a way to start off – to start a baby. What a baby that will be!

O   That is going to be a really wonderful baby.

J   Babies born from women in Satori must be marvelous babies.

O   The baby has helped her very, very much; moreover, she really believes it is like that.

J   The baby is advising her.

O   All the time inside; pure life, completely new, completely without a sin; no deviations, no ego, completely pure.

J   That is the way I felt on Tuesday, just completely pure; like a baby in the womb. Totally without deviation or sin; no responsibilities and yet responsibility for everybody.

O   Yes, that is it.

J   No contradictions; in total tune with the universe. I had never known what that meant before, being right in tune with matter – with the cosmos and nature with other people absolutely all on the same wave length – everything.

O   Bless you, John; bless you.

J   Well, I want to go back there. I don't want to be here – emoting.

O   You are going to go back all you want.

J   I'm greedy.

O   Just be a little bit patient. We need the whole group going. I know that; I saw that.

J   Now I know what my Karma was that you were talking about earlier. I didn't black out, I withstood the pain; I withstood the fear out in the outer reaches of the cosmos with Shaitan [Satan]; I stayed with him consciously and I never let go of consciousness; I stayed consciously right there. And that is what you learn; until you can go consciously into the depths of Shaitan, you can't go consciously into the depths or the heights of Satori 6. [slingshot effect – the backswing; the downswing to go up, or the trampoline effect.]

O   Yes.

J   This is where your strength comes from. Down here, way far below, the real dirty, nasty stuff that Shaitan [Satan] throws at you without your going unconscious; without going "asleep"; without forgetting. And that is why you go to sleep. It is too painful to be awake under those conditions. The pain is excruciating; the fear is incredible. The terror and pain. But unless you can stay awake down there in -6 and -12, you can't stay awake up there in +6 and +12 Satori.

O   Right.

J   OK.

O   You see, John you are saying at this very moment exactly what has to happen with someone who is making the Christ inside. You have to descend into hell. Remember what it said in the Bible, "... go down into hell." He went down into hell and then up. The same thing that you have done going down into hell.

J   But you have to stay conscious.

O   Completely. Otherwise, you are taken.

J   Well, you are either taken, or you are put back unconscious.

O   Yes, you have to stay conscious and see.

J   The way I put it myself with LSD (1964-1966) is that I had to stay responsible for myself. I am in charge of myself. No one else. So I had to stay awake and run the show. I have to run me no matter where I am. No matter what the space is, I have to stay and be a conscious being. The only thing that kept me going was that resolve to never let go of consciousness. Now with others; they get higher and suddenly they are gone. They are not in contact; not in contact with me or the reality around or with anything else. They do not remember on their return.

O   Right. They are not ready yet.

J   So, when I've been thinking that they are going into 12, they are going toward 12 and then closing up somehow. I don't know what you call this.

O   The thing is this. Because they are inexperienced, there is the ego part left; it is not taken out. They need more will.

J   What you were talking about last night – in the general session's lecture?

O   That kind of will. It is very precise. We have no definition for that will. For that energy we can say that is the will. It is not a will like a decision. It is a will that is going, going; a continuous exertion of will – will-power.

J   That is what I was talking about a few minutes ago when I was going down with Shaitan. The one thing I could hold onto was "the will to be." The willing to be no matter what has happened.

O   Yes, exactly that one.

J   The will to be, no matter what happens. OK, then that makes sense.

O   You see, it is exactly the same for the Buddha – a Satori +3 because you remember that at the very moment he did not believe anything at all. But he knew about completely, as you say, without will – without will. That will – it is very difficult to have it. We all know how difficult it is to have that will. Because at that very moment he did not believe in anything. Not even God.

J   Pure solitude.

O   Alone. Completely, pure solitude. Then the spirit came. He went inside another space and then another space until he realized "The Buddha." After that he didn't stay all the time in the Buddha position, in the Buddha state. He came down to his 24 Satori, to his 12 Satori, to his 6 Satori like us. For our living, you will see that we have to stay in 12, in 6, in 3. Not all the time in 3, not all the time in 6, not all the time in 12, not all the time in 24. We have to divide our life into the four different levels, the four different degrees. For not losing our attachment for earth, we can say.

J   I saw that during the 12 – saw it so clearly – your insistence. First of all I saw the exercises. For the first time the exercises made deep sense. When I did the Sphinx, I became the first worm to look out of the earth at the sun at the beginning of creation.

O   Will you repeat that.

J   When I did the Sphinx, I became the first worm that was in the mud to stick his head up and look and see the sun. When

I did the Cobra, I was the first snake to stick his head up out of the grass and look at the world and so on. I was a living set of what Jung calls the "archetypes." I was evolution, all the past phases. When I was doing the horizontal arm fling, I was a warrior chopping the heads off my enemies and so. Each episode was total and complete of itself. The magnificent joy of doing it. And suddenly I felt that the exercises were all turned around. The exercises are what you do when you are in Satori 12 because it is so much fun and deeply significant to do them. The exercises are not necessarily only to be done to get into 12; it is when you are in 12 that they are much fun. During the exercises, I felt a deep joyful vibration in all the body. That was an incredible experience.

O You give me such a happiness, such joy, John.

J Oscar, you really have something.

O No, you have it already. All of this, you know that.

J Yes, but I didn't know; you had to tell me; I had to come here, to Arica, Chile, and be told that I knew. He sent me to you.

O Always, John. So, the real things – Satori 24, 12, 6 and 3 for ego, are not real. They, the egos are in the place, Satori, and they say, "What is this?" more or less. It is incredible; they are in it and they don't see it. After coming down, they don't feel it. They have exactly the same feeling you referred to earlier, "over in a very nice wonderful space, but how was that?" How can he make a description of it? In most cases in which I have put them in that place, inside of Him, in the space, people don't know this and only the Essence knows it. The ego part doesn't know where it is and who helped it get into the Essence.

J   I see. In certain cases, you bypass the ego.

O   Yes.

J   You went around the ego.

O   Yes, I went around the ego, but the ego is still there. It is past the ego, around the end of it.

J   I see.

O   Those who have suffered very, very much can be incredibly cleaned of ego. I can work with these very, very fast. Some do not believe it at the moment, but they are going to go very fast. Everybody, without exception, will go into 24 very fast. You will see this. The only difference is on how long they can stay. You see, the group has very different individuals in it. It is gradually getting to be more homogeneous than it was before. Everybody understands now what I am saying. I feel that understanding is not only understanding because they are taking the baraka. Baraka is inside all the time and is completely necessary for the work. For personal work, the understanding of the deviations is absolutely essential. The work is going to be in their lives for many, many years; a long time.

J   It is amazing what you do in an hour – doing the deviations analysis.

O   It is not me, you see. I couldn't get inside of all that. That is why every night I am very tired.

J   Yes, this really is a load on you. You really are working hard these days.

O   Yes. It has to be like that, but I recover myself more or less every day. Today I went to make my Pampa [the desert exercises]; I couldn't because I have quite a pain here in the left thigh, from an accident in the martial arts combat Sunday.

J   I really want to know the way back to 12. One part of my confusion may be a deviation. Was it necessary for me to get into 12 on Tuesday, to have gone through that thing with my partner?

O   Two things; it happened at the right moment for you. Your partner is the switch that started that thing. But it was you; she was not the little switch. Immediately, you start into 12; you feel this wish for helping. This wish for everybody to share 12. So this could be the explanation. Anything could be the switch. It could be a bird. We don't know what starts 12. So, if you are at the threshold for excitation of 12 and anything, even the smallest stimulus happens, then in you go. Also, before you go into 12, you have that sensation of expansion.

J   And of movement.

O   Expansion and wanting to give or to take somebody and do it for another by some means, precisely like telling you the moment you are without ego. So that switch could be anything; a flower, a bird, the moon, a person.

J   "Moonlight on the water and a little bird singing," as you said. It is an incredible deep good sense. The little bird was there in the barraca shed singing. Sun on my eyelids, the roaring furnace of the sun. I became the sun. I went into it. Incredible power.

O   So now you are ready to go back into the Satori 12 many, many times, I'm sure. In the exercises we are going to do, I'm completely sure you will reach it again. We are going to train with the mentations. This time with the training, I'm sure each one of you are going to 12. That is very important because you realize in each mentation – Satori 12 – bump – that is going to be you.

J   It is going to depend on the mentations.

O   It is not going to depend on the mentations, but the mentations will fix it like film. Like fixing a film, so in that very moment the mentations really become angels. Angels that are helping your inside Master all the time with complete agreement with him – your inside Master with your Essence.

J   By the way, the two (guides) came on Tuesday. Remember the two guides I had told you about? They came from back on the two sides and they stayed right there.

O   Blessings on you. [Clapping his hands.] That is really marvelous.

J   It was incredibly good. [Long silence on tape. John went into Satori 12.]

O   You are going now [laughing]. The change in within the hour is something that impressed me much. [Silence. John in 12 without looking.]

J   I came back. I just went [silence] inside. [A bit of holding back because of Oscar's presence.] Still some ego there.

O   No, no, John.

J   Something is there preventing my going.

O   Perhaps. I say, perhaps. It seems to be locatable in protoanalysis; I don't think you have ego. I don't see it. But you have some kind of remembering. Think. The remembering must be something still there. There is no ego, which is the remembering that cancels so much. It is little pieces of Karma. We can be sure of this, John, that they are very small pieces. In a machine, really small pieces can stop the whole, perfect machine. Your machine is already clean. We don't know, it could be a little tack that is preventing it from running as it should run. With the protoanalysis, we can be sure. You are going to see, very fast.

J   And wash it out.

O   Wash it out, but very precisely. Then you are going to be completely sure that there is going to be no more Karma.

J   I found out what breathing is on Tuesday while in "12." It is really energy; an incredible energy. I was breathing in and it went right on down to my toes, into my head, and out to my fingers. Then up the same way. A fabulous energy flow. The tide of the universe going through me.

O   Completely, completely comes baraka.

J   The power involved was just beautifully smooth. There is none of the aspect of "lightning" anymore. Under LSD, I got a bit frightened because sometimes you would go bang, like that. There was none of that on Tuesday. It was a smooth, slow build-up.

O   It was completely yours, completely yours.

J   As if I had a throttle somewhere and was controlling it. Not me, but somebody. So it was very smooth and there was none of the lightning striking, none of that. The thing I feared. That is it! I fear what I went through on May 7, 1964, when I very nearly died; very nearly unconsciously killed myself, because I had denied what I had done. I said, "No, I couldn't do that to myself." I refused to stay conscious of what I had done. I refused awakedness.

O   There's one of your remembrances; one of your sand grains in the machine.

J   I need trust in myself while going into Satori 12; I need trust in you while going into Satori 12.

O   But you see, this trust has got to be like this, John. You have got to trust in this and you are going to see that your Essence is really one part of God. That is for real.

J   So it is not my responsibility. That is the important part.

O   No.

J   It isn't my will, it is His will.

O   It is His will. He wants it like that, so you don't need effort for that, just let it happen.

J   Wow.

O   For that you have to be completely pure, without the other thing, without the fear.

J   [Breathing deeply, he goes into Satori 12 again.] So much of what you've been saying is so obvious to me now; so obvious; so simple.

O   [In a very low voice.] Yes, that is right.

J   Where before this experience on Tuesday, it was very difficult.

O   The truth is simple.

J   It is incredible.

O   Again, in your state, if you want to say the same thing to someone else, he has to be in your state. Otherwise you have to know how to teach him in his level, in his degree.

J   I've always let them bring me down to their level in various workshops. When I was away from the groups, I would get very high, Come in and get them going, and raise their level and eventually they would pull me to the lowest level, tired and discouraged, and I would want to quit. Every so often, I'd hit on an individual who was high, who went through incredible things to bring himself up. The rest weren't prepared.

O For something, John, God has given us this life to suffer. To suffer, to learn, and to let the other ones come in the same places. Without that payment, we suffer and we pay. They don't need to. I think it is like that. If you've seen your own life, now what is going to be the best for you to do is to teach.

J I agree.

O You are here more than for you. You are here for that completely. That is why you are filled with blessings.

J There is no point in it for me unless I can teach it – the routes to 12, 6 and 3 and so forth. If you see what I mean.

O I see what you mean.

J Earlier, I came to that conclusion. Reading Vivekananda, Ramakrishna, all these other people, St. Theresa, St. John of the Cross, they didn't teach it. I have a feeling as if there is something missing in these people. They made it, they are an example. But we need more than an example. We need a method, a way. And we need teachers of that way without that particular business of putting the teachers on a big pedestal, worshiping them. This is a big mistake because if you are worshiping a human, you can't go where they are; it is misplaced worship.

O I agree.

J Misplaced reverence and awe and it is so hard to tell that to those who don't know. Every so often I catch them looking at me and I say, "Please. No, no; don't do that. If you are going to do that, see through me to who is behind me in back of me. It isn't me."

O Absolutely.

J And I don't think they will know that till they go there themselves and see that it is everywhere; that it is everybody; that it is the whole universe, this baraka, this divine grace. That is the major lesson that comes out of 12. It isn't any one person.

O That's right. That's what it's like.

J The religions have lost this, haven't they? They lost it in their power struggles.

O Now you see, John, we are really beginning a completely new culture now. The method is a really new culture. Now this method is not a channel for getting it. It is just a beginning because it is science. It is possible for us.

J One thing that bothers me is naming your method at the moment. It is not important now, but it will be later at the end of the ten months of training. What sort of name are you giving it? Is this the Sufi thing or is this something else?

O   We call it always "The School."

J   People want a label. The Sufi name in the United States has a lot of prestige, Karma, whatever, among the youngsters who count. We want to make it something entirely new. I don't know, I'm just raising questions. I don't want answers.

O   It is better for us, John, that the name is something new because the teaching is completely new. If we confuse our names, for instance with Sufism, everybody is going prepared for that way. Let us make it something new. One Sufi, a dervish, was wearing this patchwork cloak. He was supposed to be in a very high level except he was in this patchwork cape. You didn't see anything really special. In talking with him I saw only one thing. I said [about his cape], "Why do you use this?" He said, "Because I am in a state of complete and total humility." Immediately, I said to him, "Why do you show it? (End of tape.)

For the next few weeks, I continued my work on the deviations of my mentations and in general followed the analysis philosophy that was laid down by Oscar. "Positive states are natural, simple, easy, obvious, and continuous. Anything that brings one out of Satori is ego." In other words, ego is that which reduces love, joy, conscious awareness. "It is important work to reduce the ego."

After my first two experiences in state +12, the work started to find out how to get back into those beautiful places. I felt at this point that my work had finally started. There were various barriers and evasions that come into this problem.

My next major sortie into state "+12" country occurred in the desert. Each member of the group was programmed to spend a week in the desert, alone in a small A-frame hut. As the first week-long member, I spent five days and nights, three of which were in a new (for me) area of "+12."

As I watched the sunset the second evening, I suddenly saw a three-layered cloud formation over the Pacific ocean of extreme brilliance and immense beauty with a vertical shaft of brilliant white light. The formation was a triple cross. I started to cry, lonely at first, for me. I went with the grief. It changed to grief-joy combined and it was for all humans – first on this planet, later throughout the galaxy.

This crying "+12" continued through three days including a visit by Oscar. During his visit, I did not shut down the crying or the grief-joy and shared it with him. Later he called this a special region, "making the Christ, the green qutub" in state +12.

Chapter 16
STATE +6: THE POINT AS SELF

Each of the positive states, including +6, is best understood by going to the next higher state and also by knowing the next lower state. If one has been to +3, one cannot move into +6 without knowing it. Otherwise, one may think that +6 is merely an extension of +12. If one has not had the experiences of +6, it probably is a good idea to memorize a map having to do with +6 by separating it out from +12, + 24, and +3.

Here above all other places that we have discussed so far, the Beliefs Unlimited exercise applies. I derived these statements from my experience in the tank work in which I went to +6.

> *"In the province of the mind, what I believe to be true, is true or becomes true within certain limits to be found experientially and experimentally. These limits are further beliefs to be transcended."*

Let's review +6, +6 is that state in which one focuses one's consciousness down to a very small point. How small the point is is a matter of choice that one makes depending upon where one wants to go. One makes sure that one carries into the point one's memories, one's feelings, one's thinking processes, one's maps of these places, one's total perceptions of what is going on around one. One carries all of one's 48 maps into the point, without words, as directing experiences.

One leaves behind totally the screen of words that one normally carries around in 48 and +24 and that one has partially left behind in +12. By the time that one reaches +6, there are no words, there are no sentences, there is no syntax, no grammar, no language, there are no numbers, there are no quantitative scales, there are no computations, there is no usual logic, usual thinking, there is no ordinary reality. One is totally immersed in a nonordinary reality, in a nonordinary being, in a nonordinary kind of direct perception, of direct experience and of direct storage of these in memory.

After the near-lethal accident I described earlier in this book, I moved into state +6, into a particular golden light space. I met two guides, who were points of consciousness, warmth, love, and radiance, even as I was. We had no need for word communication, no need for the usual planetside trip communication because each of us had direct perception of the other's feeling state and thinking process. We could exchange information directly from mind to mind without the intervening need of the usual physical means. After this level 6 experience, I then recaptured the three times that I had done it earlier at ages twenty-two, seven and five. I was able to reproduce state +6 in the tank with LSD in the 1964-1966 series of experiments.

Once one has moved into the point, become the point, one can move down into the body, into other people's heads or bodies, or out over the planet, or into outer space, into the galaxy, into the cosmos. As long as one holds together as one identity, a single point, one remains in state +6 no matter how far out, no matter how deep down one is going. If one is still an identifiable point functioning on its own, even though it is being programmed by other entities, one is in state +6. I found this a very convenient way of distinguishing +12 from +6 and +6 from +3. In +12 the body is still present; in +6 it is not. In +6 one is still oneself, more or less; in +3 one loses that self and becomes an Essence, one of the universal pilots of vehicles.

The old psychic textbooks gave directions for getting into +6 by creating an astral body and an astral cord so that one can stay connected back with the physical body. This is excess baggage that one does not need. This is using up some of one's computation machinery in a narcissistic security operation. The more efficient means of travel is in the point, without the artificial construction of a needless body on these levels (cf. R. A. Monroe's account, bibliography).

The same consideration holds true for the entities that one meets in state +6. There is no point in clothing them with the bodies of angels or other types of human projections. This might use up your store of computational ability, which is needed for much more profound tasks on +6.

It is on +6 that one may begin to realize one's own eternal nature. Here it is that one may come upon one's previous lives. One may come upon information about the future – probable futures, or perhaps a secure knowledge about how long one's body or vehicle is going to last and under what circumstances it will die.

It is here that one experiences pure cosmic love with all of its dispassionate interest and its unequivocal effectiveness. With the two guides I was aware of their fantastic power and of their beginning to influence me toward understanding of the universal laws of the universe, including those of my own being. I found them to be very tolerant but absolutely ruthless teachers. It was they who sent me to -3 (vibrational level 768) (see Chapter 5) in order to teach me that I did not need negative states at all. They put me in the most negative conceivable state – more negative than anything I could have possibly imagined or constructed within my own self, my biocomputer; yet not so negative that I couldn't remember what had happened when I came back.

On +6, as you may have gathered by now, one can construct bodies, can construct anything that one wishes to construct. If you will refer back to the account of my -3 experiences (768) in the chapter "Guided Tour to Hell" by the time I got back to robot level, I was in +6; I was a point observer watching the two programmers and the robots and the computed maze. Here the sign, the motivational sign of the space, was shifting from minus to plus. I was moving from -3 to +6 in these experiences.

In the hypnosis experience with Helen Bonnie and Ken Godfrey in Topeka, when I "traveled" to California, I was in +6; the episode of the chandelier and of the burning bedcover were both done in +6. In each of these cases I was a point source observing what was going on.

In my first two LSD trips, I took various trips through my body. Here I was also in +6, a point observer moving down through the body.

As one's experience with +6 develops, it becomes a much broader space than one conceived in the first instance.

In Chile during the state +12 experience in the early part of August, I heard the roar that can take place as one is moving from +12 into +6. I pulled back into +12 and stayed in my body as a totally functioning conscious body rather than shrinking down to the point. Later I had an unequivocal experience in +6.

Our assignment for that particular day had been to put on our hoods. These are typical monks' hoods made out of brown cloth, which we would put over our heads and use to isolate ourselves visually from our surroundings. You cannot see out of them.

I put on my hood and went out into a field to pray in the late afternoon sunshine. I had previously argued with Oscar about the efficacy of prayer, saying that I had prayed as a child and that I had abandoned the practice. He just said, "Try it."

As I knelt, in the field, isolated in my hood,* praying, suddenly the two guides appeared on each side of me. A shaft of warmth, radiance, and love came down from the sun. The two guides and I fused; the fused being of the three of us moved up the shaft of light toward the sun.

I felt warm, wanted, identified with the guides, completely integrated with the universe. In spite of this fusion, I maintained

---

* The hood is a visual physical isolation device; the isolation box mentioned elsewhere is an acoustic, visual, and tactile isolator; the Isolation tank removes all these, plus antigravity forces.

my own identity, went into the sun, then came back to my body. And yet, I had never left my body. There was a connection up to +6 with the help of the two guides and the maintenance of the body itself. I had the consciousness of being both at +6 and at the body simultaneously.

It was this type of integration of the various levels that I was striving for under Oscar's tutorship. The maintenance of the body in state +12, while developing the point as self in +6 simultaneously, was the kind of thing that I had hoped to do and finally achieved through the prayer that day in the field.

As has been reported by practically every author attempting to describe experiences on +6, it is very difficult to come back through the screen of words between +12 and +24 and carry with one appropriate descriptions of what happens. The process of direct knowing, of direct knowledge without intervening thinking processes on +6 is very hard to describe in words because one is using the screen of words to describe that which is beyond the screen of words. I suspect that William James's "filmiest of screens" is just that: a screen of words describing thinking processes that are totally inappropriate in the other realities. One exercise to get one beyond the screen of words and directly and rapidly into +6 is "I am not the biocomputer; I am not the programmer, I am not the program, I am not the programming, I am not that which is programmed." If one's concepts of one's own biocomputer processes include these five regions and if one can make the statements real, one can quite quickly separate oneself off from the screen of words, from the body, from the biocomputer, from the planetside trip. With this technique, I have found that it is relatively natural for me to make short trips into state +6.

I have found that it is best when using this particular technique to stay fairly close to the body and watch what happens. Usually I end up about a foot to three feet above the top of my head watching the biocomputer and the self-metaprogrammer running the show in the body down there below me. Sometimes this can have quite humorous results.

At a certain point at the trip in Chile, I was doing an ego reduction with another man. He had found a bit of my ego and I went up quite automatically into Satori +6 yet holding in +24 and +12. The part of me in +6 took a look around and saw that part of him was peaking into +6 but that he didn't know it. I came back down and reported this to him, including one sentence on having met him before in a previous life. He apparently wasn't aware of the part of himself that went to +6 nor the part in +12, nor the part in +24, "He" was in 48. He became extremely angry, going into 96 immediately upon hearing me talk about previous lives in which his self-metaprogrammer does not believe; he broke off our contact.

Another time, I was doing some of the group exercises at night; the ones called Kind rhythm and I went into +6 partially, still maintaining connection with the body. This is a rather difficult exercise in the beginning. One says a mantram, moves one's hand in a definite pattern, moves the energy of the body in definite ways and moves one's consciousness into a rock in one's hand. While I was doing all of these things, suddenly I pulled out. I got above my body. I watched the self-metaprogrammer run the body, and learned that I didn't have to do anything about this at all, that it was all pretty much an automatic program. I could sit up there and watch the whole program take place and sort of run the show. I added other things to what the body and the self-metaprogrammer were doing until there were about 25 things going at once, instead of 5.

This experience showed me that the closer one gets to Essence, the real pilot of the vehicle, the less complicated the trip really is and the easier it is to carry out the programs necessary to the planetside trip. The Essence, as the true pilot, is in such a position that he can tune in on all the control positions of the self-metaprogrammer, of the biocomputer, of the body, and of all the external realities simultaneously. Thus, I suddenly realized that in state +6 one is identified with Essence and yet the self-metaprogrammer is still present under the behest of Essence. This smooth moving of one's center of consciousness from the self-metaprogrammer into the Essence watching the self-metaprogrammer is the key to understanding state +6. Once one's center of consciousness is in the Essence, then anything can happen having to do with the body, with the self-metaprogrammer, the planetside trip, or, these can be kept behind and you can go elsewhere. Suddenly I realized that all Essences are connected to one another on level 6 and are in communication whether one's self knows this or not. They also share past histories of each self. There is no hiding anything from the other Essences. Essence, by its very nature, is a shared totality of consciousness, warmth, love, and memory. The cosmic energy flows through the biological organism and through the Essence as a valve for cosmic love, cosmic energy or baraka.

It is extremely important that one clarify one's concepts in this region. As one clarifies the concepts, the pathways to +6 are purified and facilitated. As one's machinery becomes perfected, one can move into +6 more easily. As one de-emphasizes and reduces those programs which keep one out of +6, it becomes easier and easier to get there for whatever time is practical.

The boundary between +6 and +3 can be understood as the

boundary between all Essences and one's own particular Essence. As one moves more and more into one's own Essence, one suddenly discovers there is a strong connection from one's own Essence into all other Essences in the universe. The first time one makes that discovery, one moves into the next state, +3, the classical Satori-Samadhi.

Chapter 17

STATE +3: CLASSICAL SATORI; THE ESSENCE AS ONE OF THE CREATORS

The state +3 (which corresponds to the classical use of the term "Satori") is the most difficult of the states to deal with in the sense that it is the least familiar and furthest from our consensus reality. It is the space close to death of the vehicle. It is the place to which people fear to go because they may not come back to the body. I had been to +3 only once or twice in my previous experiences, and the trip to Chile was based upon the fact that I wanted to go to a clear, conscious +3 and find out what was there.

From the state +12 in August until the first occurrence of state +3 in November, I had a lot of planetside trip work to do. A lot of this was physical, a lot of it was mental, and a lot of it was social and interpersonal. I was to spend five days and nights in the desert alone, going through the grief-joy space for a period of seventy-two hours, breaking open my feeling center in the chest.

I was to settle my differences with my dyadic partner. We finally agreed, while both were in a state of 48, that she would move and live somewhere else. Within twenty-four hours of that agreement, I was able to get into my first really solid, strong, conscious contact with state +3.

I'll quote from my notes from that period. For Wednesday, 24 Nov. 1970 4 a.m. "Chaos started, [it] pulled my being apart both in the external realities and in the internal realities. It was necessary that I center in my Kath in my isolation box.*

"Suddenly, I was in -3 briefly. I was in the grips of the paranoid cosmic conspiracy as a small program in the big computer, but this time I knew where I was. I recentered myself by accepting me as part of the universe, as part of the cosmos. Suddenly I become one of the programmers of the cosmic computer, as is a god joined to gods under God. The void and beyond us. We run the universe of all beings and matter, even those not yet awake. Awake, we are outside the cosmic computer, no longer in it. We are the programmers of it; we are not programs in it anymore (we are "off the wheel of life"). I have immense joy in joining the controllers and being tightly coupled with their network. The cosmic computer was over there. We were over here running it. In turn, we were programmed by the will of God, the ultimate programmer in whom we worked. This was a high, interlocked, gold energy universe of being. I felt, saw, knew a crystal which was the programs of the Essence. This crystal was the wired-in programs of the cosmic computer, shining with gold energy, continuously describing the limits of the programmer group's operations. These programs were as follows:

---

* A box 2 feet wide, 2 feet deep, 7 feet long with a mattress in it and a cover. You lower the lid after you climb in so as to be isolated in darkness and silence.

1. 'Holy Law' is the limits within which we work, think, feel and are; (it is) a shining program boundary around our operational space;

2. 'Perfection' is the computer doing perfect programs and programming perfectly all being, all matter, all consciousness.

3. 'Holy Work' is our activity and our being, the Creators, the Programmers.

4. 'Freedom' is doing the operations with joy within our defined limits, We are free of being within the computer, free to do the programming, free to be metaprogrammed by God's Will.

5. 'Holy Love' is what we receive, is what we give as we do our perfect thing. As we are linked, so we are loved and love-objectively, realized, essentially, purely.

6. 'Omniscience' is a sure transparent knowledge of the whole transparent computer, who runs it, who runs us, the group; knowledge of the void out of which all of this came; the links with the void.

7. 'Sobriety' inside these operations, is that state of me that is reverence, love, staying within known limits. There is a lack of fantasy about truth. There is knowing truth directly.

8. 'Equanimity' is a very high state in which everything is balanced in supreme joy, and functions are smoothly done with the others; the power of the cosmos flows through us.

9. 'Holy Truths' – all of this plus God Himself is the truth with certitude.

10   'Veracity' – I live my truths fully, truly.

11   'Courage': There is no sign of doubt or fear or -3;
     I am sustained by my strength, our strength.

12   'Detachment' is being one of the programmers
     outside of the cosmic computer, programming
     as it needs programming, objectively,
     realistically, in tune with the creative flow.

13   'Innocence' – the innocence of childhood, accepting what
     is happening with dedication and without question
     – being in the cosmic group without question."

This description of parts of the wired-in program of the cosmic computer, plus the over-riding metaprogrammer with which the group of programmers were running it, we called the crystal of the Essence. Oscar had given us these ideas in the form of nine-sided figures called eneagrams, each idea being at one point of the eneagram. I saw how this was all organized in the cosmic computer, in me, in the group that ran it.

As I was coming back from +3 this time there were many, many choices. "I was spread out over all of the routes back, 10 million of them. Then 10,000, then 100, then 10, then there was coalescence into one channel, into my former body, with the sense that I had done this many, many times before in other bodies, in other lives, in other places in the universe.

"In the cosmic computer are all repetitions, all tape loops necessary to keep the cosmos going; the noise, sight, sounds, feelings, rhythms are obvious and full.

"I then went through another experience. I saw myself, me, on January 11, 1969, in -3; I saw me then, a little program; a lesson taught and learned. In that computer, in the conspiracy computer, all is evil because I am forced to be programmed; all is senseless.

"The real cosmic computer, the one at +3, was changed to 'Everything is significant and powerful to me, I am not afraid.' As I received strength, I would pass it on to the others with me.

"This experience was uniquely me-integrated into Oscar Ichazo's ideas and maps. Plus 3, for me, is not a peaceful place, but it is a high energy rewarding experience."

About ten days after this experience I made a discovery that was to lead me back to +3 even more powerfully, more centered and with greater strength. This discovery may be useful in a more general sense than for just my purposes. I quote from Saturday, December 5, in my notes. "I am not my opinion of myself, I am not anything I can describe to me. I am only a part of a large system that cannot describe itself fully; therefore I relax and I am in the point source of consciousness, of delight, of mobility, in the inner spaces. My tasks do not include describing me nor having an opinion about the system in which I live, biological or social or dyadic. I hereby drop that 'responsibility.'

"I am much more than I can conceive or judge me to be. Any negative or positive opinions I have of me are false fronts, headlines, limited and unnecessary programs written on a thin paper blowing about and floating around in the vastness of inner spaces."

As G. Spencer Brown says in *The Laws of Form*,* p. 105, "We may take it that the world is undoubtedly itself (i.e., is indistinct from itself), but, in any attempt to see itself, as an object, it must, equally undoubtedly act so as to make itself distinct from and therefore false to itself. In this condition, it will always partially elude itself." And so with each one of us, "In this sense, in respect to its own information, the universe must expand to escape the telescopes through which we, who are it, are trying to capture it, which is us."

My notes continue: "Therefore, if I feel bad or euphoric, about me, I am falsely attributing omnipotence to a part of the system as if it knew the whole, which it cannot. Negative brain systems are only part of the system I live in, as are the positive ones. Negative system stimulation constricts me through aversion; positive system stimulation constricts me through attachment.

"Being neither positive nor negative, the high energy neutral state 48 allows penetration into unknown spaces without attachment or aversion.

"This view seems to conflict with state +12 (samadhi sananda). It does not, if one allows experience of the positive state *without attachment to it*. If I allow reoccurrence of +12 without trying for it, I am not attached. Plus 12 is a natural, simple, easy obvious state. When out of it, I am being judging in one sense, by keeping myself out of it; the natural, simple, easy, and obvious escapes me when I separate from it. If I am it, I am not separate from it. If I chase it, I separate into the chaser and the chased. If I am it, I am it and nothing else."

---

* London: Geo. Allen & Unwin, 1989.

With this preparation, on Sunday, December 13, for the second time I moved into state +3. I started out by riding through the body power and body sex spaces without giving into either one. I allowed the equivalent of a grand mal seizure to take place while maintaining full consciousness. Somehow, now, I could stand this seizure-like activity far better than I had ever been able to before.

"Suddenly I saw myself in the corner of the room fighting against the universal laws, not wanting to live inside the limits I had found. I suddenly saw that this was Shaitan (Satan) crouching in the corner. In other words, the devil is only me fighting against the universe's laws. As soon as I saw this, I was suddenly precipitated into the power and creation space of state +3."

My notes continue: "I am a thin layer of all those beings on 3, mingling, connected with one another in a spherical surface around the whole known universe. Our 'backs' are to the void. We are creating energy, matter and life at the interface between the void and all known creation. We are facing into the known universe, creating it, filling it. I am one with them; spread in a thin layer around the sphere with a small, slightly greater concentration of me in one small zone. I feel the power of the galaxy pouring through me. I am following the program, the conversion program of void to space, to energy, to matter, to life, to consciousness, to us, the creators. From nothing on one side to the created everything on the other. I am the creation process itself, incredibly strong, incredibly powerful.

"This time there is no flunking out, no withdrawal, no running away, no unconsciousness, no denial, no negation, no fighting against anything. I am 'one of the boys in the engine room pumping creation from the void into the known universe; from the unknown to the known I am pumping.'

"There is no trace of -3, no Shaitan, no trampoline or springboard effect. This state, place, space, galactic universe, shell of +3 is n-dimensional and is multilevel, specifiable.

"I am coming back from level +8. There are a billion choices of where to descend back down. I am conscious down each one of the choices simultaneously. Finally I am in my own galaxy with millions of choices left, hundreds of thousands on my own solar system, tens of thousands on my own planet, hundreds in my own country and then suddenly I am down to two, one of which is this body. In this body I look back up, see the choice-tree above me that I came down.

"Did I, this Essence, come all the way back down to this solar system, this planet, this place, this body, or does it make any difference? May not this body be a vehicle for any Essence that came into it? Are not all Essences from level +3 universal, equal, anonymous, and equally able? Instructions for this vehicle are in it for each Essence to read and absorb on entry. The new pilot navigator reads his instructions in storage and takes over, competently operating this vehicle. (The instruction book for this vehicle is in the glove compartment.)

"So I am a combination of Essence plus vehicle, plus its computer, plus the self-metaprogrammer as a unit. The other creators on level +3 are from all over the universe, not just planet earth and the solar system. Since each is a replaceable universal unit, anonymous, it can be working on +3 or on a planetside trip vehicle or elsewhere in the universe as needed, always connected to all of its fellows. The only thing that prevents me from knowing my Essence all of the time is a screen of programs preventing my seeing."

I spent about six hours on this work at state +3. This seemed to be the culmination of my work in Chile. Various details were cleared up and on the 25th, 26th, and 27th of January, I did a three-day prayer in solitude following Oscar's program. The point was, he explained, to reach divine guidance as to whether we should continue working with the group or whether something else was in store for us. During the three days of solitude and prayer, I finally received a very definite feeling, as if an instruction, that I leave Oscar for now; there was something that I was going to do in the United States.

It seemed to me at that time that one of the jobs that I was to do was find others who already know +12, +6 and +3. I did not realize at that point how hard this is. However, I also knew that I had to go back to somehow find, or at least to look for, my female counterpart. The day I got back, February 7, 1977, I did a series of exercises and, while in Zen sitting, got into a very special state which was an integration of +24, +12, +6 and +3.

"I stay centered and grounded by effort in the Kath and put the Kath in the earth. There are multiple planes of being, of energy, intersecting at very high energy through my body's vertical axis. I am in Zen kneeling position. A line from my Ma'h, my Path, my Oth, my Kath intersected all the planes (see scale of vibration levels). I feel that if I move the slightest bit out of this line, I will fall into one or another of the many spaces available. If I keep the line vertical and do the truth mudra (backs of hands on knees, index finger and thumb forming a circle, other three fingers extended) I stay centered.

"Slippage into other positive and negative levels begins to occur at first. Then with the mudra, I hold on to the line. Amazing energy sweeps through me; there are direct connections to +6 and +3, known and felt without going out of the body. The main feeling is "If I fight the laws, I slip into the meaningless program of -6, -3" – then I am nothing but a small program. When I accept the laws, I am in divine cosmic love. I can take the energy, and stay centered on the line.

"Immediately after this, I experienced a liquid gold-red light pouring out of the cosmos onto and down through me, with immense love and gratitude flowing around every cell of me. I became illuminated and enlightened and immensely happy."

Two weeks after the multilevel experience, on Sunday, February 21, at a party I met my soul mate, the other half (female) of my Essence, as it were.

Chapter 18

DYADIC SATORI: UNITY IN A COUPLE

With the training that I had received in state +3 and level -3, I realized that I still had a lot of Karma to deal with having to do with my relations with a woman; with my dyad. I came back to the United States from Chile to do this work. In Arica, for me it was very unsatisfactory working in a dyad. The group work and the individual work were so demanding that there was hardly any time for dyadic work.

I don't want to give the impression that individual work, group work, or dyadic work take precedence, one over the other. Some of the couples in Arica in the training worked on all three fronts at once. Now I am sure that if a couple is well matched, they can carry out the whole program simultaneously without the divisions that I had.

With the fusion on +3, I could accept fusion on the planetside trip – fusion I fought against before. I had felt that if I fused with another, she would take over and I would lose my initiative. This was no longer true. I knew that the vehicles themselves, hers and mine, were each independent, that the Essences were already fused. The work to be accomplished for the self-metaprogrammers in each one of the biocomputers, male and female, was to join one another, to interlock happily.

In the past I had always assumed that genital joining was all that one could achieve in a couple. I had had a few brief, very short experiences of joining a woman in ways higher than just the genital way. I had not yet met an appropriate woman. Just before I met Antonietta (Toni), I had just given up all hope of ever finding the right woman. She, also, had just given up finding an appropriate man. At that point we met. Giving up, allowing, no longer striving for something, allowing it to happen, going with the flow, it happened to each of us.

The meeting took place at a house in the hills near Hollywood at 1:30 a.m. I had been invited to a party after an Alan Watts lecture at this house. The car I was riding in had a flat tire – hence the late hour. Alan had left the party – in fact, there were few survivors. As I walked in the front door I noted a dark-haired woman sitting on the floor in the large entrance hall. After meeting the host and the few remaining guests, I went over to her.

As I moved closer, I felt and saw her aura of love and beneficent influence. Her face is striking and unusual: there is an eaglelike quality to her gray eyes and classic nose – a sharp penetrating dispassionate, analytical quality, with awakedness and lively interest showing frankly and directly. I felt her centered, grounded, trusting, confident self sitting there watching me approach her from across the room.

I sat down with her, looked directly at her looking directly at and into me. Instantly I knew her and she knew me. We went into a sparkling cosmic love place together. I asked her name, age, attachments and all the necessary "48" information – she did the same.

I felt we had been together in previous lives and said "Where have you been for the last five hundred years?" She answered, "In training."

We both found this same feeling – our lives had been a training for each of us to meet the other. We were to meet to do a work of some sort together – work yet to be defined.

Four days later I went to a party at her house. We began to realize our new reality, a real together reality. We have not been apart for more than a few hours since.

Once Toni was asked by a friend how she'd changed since we'd formed our dyad. She told about grieving (joyfully) for her former self, saying, "She wasn't such a bad sort alone; now that she's in the unity of the dyad, she's completed, us."

The ruthless nature of cosmic love (baraka) has been reshown to us in our dyad. Cosmic love loves and teaches you whether you like it or not; it has an inevitability, a fullness of taking over, a fateful joyous quality that spreads and brings others to you, teaching through you. Each of us feel this strongly, now.

This meeting with my soulmate, with all of its overtones of joy, acceptance, and happiness, heralded the beginning of a new attack of ego (Karma). As Oscar had said in Arica, "You have dealt with most of your ego. There are just a few grains of sand [and I added, "of diamond hardness"] in the perfect machine – now all you have to do is clean that machine and it will run smoothly in Satori."

In joining up with Toni, I discovered that the sand was once again in myself. Luckily both of us were strong enough so that we could work on this together. This mutual cooperative venture, to clean up our machines together, is in the essential nature of our dyad.

She allowed me to teach her about many things she already knew about Satori from her own experiences. I taught her the Gym and the mentations. She and I began to teach other people in my workshops.

She had many friends before I showed up; I felt that I had joined her "village." She has an amazing appreciation of humanity as a whole. Her friends cover a much wider spectrum of personality types than I had previously allowed that close to me. She taught me tolerance, she taught me that behind a façade of an alien sort, there is the same basic human being. She taught me that the planetside trip is a beautiful place; that shared +12 is far superior to a narcissistic, lonely +12; that a dyadic +6 can move into universal +6 and thus go to +3.

Between us we found new routes to +12, +6 and +3; very easy, simple, continuous, and obvious routes which I cannot yet fully articulate.

The center of the Cyclone, in the deepest analysis I have yet done, is the quiet peaceful creating meeting place for all of us, connected in the Cosmic Network of Essences.

Epilogue

It is necessary for me to state clearly where I am in regard to this autobiography as of the time of completing it. I have moved beyond where I was when I experienced the recorded events and beyond where I was when I wrote about the experiences. Inevitably one moves. Nothing that I have written is final, completed or closed.

As I stated in *The Human Biocomputer*, I am a scientific explorer, nothing more, nothing less. My loyalties are to objective exploration, objective experiment, and repeatable testable observations. I value above all else verifiable operational theory, which gives one insight into universal nature and our own inner natures. My tests are pragmatic empirical with minimal necessity for faith in the generalizations of others. I abhor dogmas and the dogmatic doctrinaire "unique truth" of the esoteric schools. I have no room for zealots or fanatics, or the tyranny over the individual of anaclitic grouping.

Man's future lies with aware courageous informed knowledgeable experienced individuals in a loosely coupled exploratory communicating network. Such a network exists and functions beautifully with gentle effectiveness throughout this planet. I suspect it extends farther than our earth, but this is yet to be publicly demonstrated unequivocally beyond the private experience of myself and of others.

My own skepticism is intact – please keep yours. Skepticism is a necessary instrument in the exploration of the unknown. Humor is even more necessary, especially in regard to one's own self and one's observations and records. Full dispassionate detachment implies cosmic comedy with each of us a fun-loving player. Cosmic love is ruthlessly loving: whether you like it or not it loves you, teaches you, teases you, plays with you, surprises you.

It is all too easy to preach "go with the flow." The main problem is identifying what the flow is, here and now. Is a pattern I think I see "the flow" or is this my limited beliefs operating on insufficient data abstracting a false flow? One's maps and metamaps measure the flows – one's resistance measures the direction and the velocity. Without clear maps one cannot even see the flow, much less go with it. Even when one truly goes with the flow one had better touch shore or bottom once in a while to be sure one isn't just floating in the stagnant waters of secure beliefs.

Sometime the flow leads into rapids and whirlpools – here I suggest following the advice of the fold-boaters; when your boat turns over in the rapids, kick free of it and swim toward the light. No matter what happens, no matter who gives what advice, swim toward the light of your own truth.

In the book I illustrate a general principle of living and being. It is a principle I wrote out in *The Human Biocomputer*. Here I revise and enlarge it. In a scientific exploration of any of the inner realities, I follow the following metaprogrammatic steps:

1   Examine whatever one can of where the new spaces are, what the basic beliefs are to go there.

2   Take on the basic beliefs of that new area as if true.

3   Go into the area fully aware, in high energy, storing everything, no matter how neutral, how ecstatic, or how painful the experiences become.

4   Come back here, to our best of consensus realities, temporarily shedding those basic beliefs of the new area and taking on those of the investigator impartially dispassionately objectively examining the recorded experiences and data.

5   Test one's current models of this consensus reality.

6   Construct a model that includes this reality and the new one in a more inclusive succinct way. No matter how painful such revisions of the models are, be sure they include both realities.

7   Do not worship, revere, or be afraid of any person, group, space, or reality. An investigator, an explorer, has no room for such baggage.

I used this system many times in my life; in the early isolation work, in the tank work with LSD, in the Esalen experiences, in the Chile work. Each time I made what reconnaissance I could, entered the new area with enthusiasm and as openly as I could, took on the local beliefs as if true, experienced the region intensely, and finally moved out again, shedding the beliefs while critically examining the data and reprogramming my theories.

In my own way I have found that deep understanding is the best path for me into the unknown, the "highest" states of consciousness. I fully expect to continue to pursue this path. I consider everything I have written as transitional – as the exploration deepens and widens so we will be able to do a better job of mapping and exploring and further mapping.

As of today I have found no final answers, I am intent on continuing the search. Am I just the leader of 100 billions of connected cells? If so, who elected me leader? Where did the cells come from? If I am more than just the net result of 100 billions of cells living cooperatively, where did I come from?

The miracle is that the universe created a part of itself to study the rest of it, that this part, in studying itself, finds the rest of the universe in its own natural inner realities.

Acknowledgments

For this 45th Anniversary edition of Dr. John C. Lilly's classic, *The Center of the Cyclone*, I would like to thank Graham Talley for leading the way to this publication, as an editor, and as the publisher. Also at Coincidence Control Publishing, Josh Fitz, Marshall Hammond, and Jeanine Bocci provided their unwavering assistance and expertise throughout the process in bringing this edition forward.

Glenn and Lee Perry, John's esteemed colleagues continue to inspire at the forefront of the global floating renaissance. Additional thanks are extended to Lee Perry for contributing to this edition with her writing. I commend John Lilly's great friend, Adam Trombly, for his visionary interpretation of this work's influence.

Thanks also to James Bigtwin and Kate Greene. Bigtwin created johnclilly.com in 1996 and has faithfully managed it the past 21 years. Iven Lourie at Gateways Books is commended for his publications relating to John Lilly's floatation tank research and the benefits of sensory deprivation: *The Deep Self* and *Tanks for the Memories*, as well as *The Mind of the Dolphin*.

2017 will see the publication of the first compendium of Dr. Lilly's work, titled *In The Province of the Mind – The John C. Lilly*

Centennial Reader, edited by Gerard Houghton and Craig Inglis, and published by Synergetic Press. 2018 is the projected release date for the first formal biography of John Lilly's life, written by Joshua Horwitz, author of the award winning *War of the Whales*.

Gratitude is extended to John's many friends and family around the globe, including: Barbara Lilly, Sophie Mackenzie Smith, Molly Jordan Koch, Jeff Bridges, Jackson Browne, Lucy Casado, James Chellis, Divyam Preaux, Joichi Ito at MIT Media Lab, Arielle Edleman, Napier Marten, James Hamilton, Jim Ed Norman, Ann Holbrook Moss, Jerry Moss, Michael Butler, George and Pat Milman, Thomas Welch, Esq., Vicki Marshall, and Ashkahn Jahromi at Float On.

Finally, thanks to Henry Lowood and Roberto Trujillo at Stanford University Green Library Special Collections for their efforts involving the John C. Lilly Papers, archived at the university.

"In the province of the mind, there are no limits…"

Philip Hansen Bailey
John C. Lilly Research Institute
Executor, Estate of John C. Lilly

IN THE PROVINCE OF MY MIND

Reading this book again, now that floating is happening all over Planet Earth, has opened an extraordinary perspective on the passion in which I have been involved these last 40 years. I have introduced many thousands of people to their first float and witnessed as many varieties of human responses – laughter, tears, wonder, surprise, presence...

I am totally consumed by the idea that John Lilly presents early in his introduction to *Center of the Cyclone*. Maybe I never read the introduction before. I don't always read them.

I was a special education teacher with a class of "special" students that the schools had some difficulties serving, and it looked as if I was having some difficulties too. My first week in that classroom let me know that I was up against the masters of classroom mischief. Instruction from the school administration: "Keep them out of the office."

I was a good teacher, so I knew I was on the hunt for HELP and only hoped I recognized it when I saw it. "Special" HELP came from a psychologist friend getting his master's degree in "Use of the The Isolation Tank," invented by Dr. John Lilly. I told him I didn't know anything about Dr. Lilly, and I was looking for help with a very difficult classroom – could this be it?

He said, "Yes."

I said yes to being a subject in a research study about the benefits using a floatation tank, and that's how I got started.

So, back to Center of the Cyclone. This is what John Lilly says in his introduction in 1971:

> "It is my firm belief that the experience of higher states of consciousness is necessary for survival of the human species. If we can each experience at least the lower levels of Satori, there is hope that we won't blow up the planet or otherwise eliminate life as we know it. If every person on the planet, especially those in power in the establishments, can eventually reach high levels of states regularly, the planet will be run with relatively simple efficiency and joy."

There are many means of reaching these states. Among them, floating in solitude – isolation – confinement – the floatation tanks. The atmosphere created in float centers is generated by the practice of floating.

I believe that our industry has the potential to support this growth and act as an example of organizations run from higher consciousness, with a goal of spreading floating far and wide while helping each other.

After 40+ years in this industry, I have come to embrace in my heart John Lilly's most well known statement: "What one believes to be true, either is true or becomes true in one's mind, within limits to be determined experimentally and experientially. These limits are beliefs to be transcended."

Float more!

Lee Perry, Samadhi Tank Co.
Grass Valley, CA
December 2016

TOWARD EQUILIBRATION

I first set eyes on this book right after it was published in 1972. When I began to peruse it, I was immediately disarmed by the directness of the writing. Here was Dr. John Lilly, a physician and scientist of some considerable standing, who, along with a handful of other brave members of his generation, was breaking the taboo against the exploration of the vastness of our own basic nature, speaking very directly to matters that many other scientists and academics studiously (and often tediously) avoid.

Writing in intimate and honest terms about his life, his experimentations with psychedelics and consciousness, and even his own neuroses, John Lilly got my attention. His insights into his own character were illustrative of a remarkable human being who had not descended into corporate hell at the age of thirty or forty. He wasn't "in it to win it." He was just unequivocally committed to his path, however it unfolded, missteps and all.

After I read *Center of the Cyclone,* and as years became decades, I continued to devour all of John's other books, not with the reverence of a follower, but with deep respect, gratitude, and appreciation for the voice of someone of great intelligence who cast away everything superfluous in order to wake up. His was the testimony of someone who had entered into a path of awakening beyond the completely artificial barriers of organized stupidity as a social norm.

I was enthralled back then and even now, over forty years later, I am still grateful for his unabashed exposition. I am certain that many of his contemporaries were offended by John and expressed themselves (usually to his back) as such. But many others were encouraged and fortified in their own explorations and discoveries by John's journey beyond conventional, ritualized unconsciousness.

I hope that new readers of this book will appreciate just how challenging it was, and still is, to move beyond the quagmire of the status quo. The brave souls who try to open the doors of perception often find that the bastions of subjective inertia and cultural stagnation do everything in their power to slam those doors shut. The funny thing is that once those doors are truly opened, the explorers realize that they were never framed by any real walls or limitations. What we find in *The Center of the Cyclone* is a confession of a door truly opening, of recognizing and transcending the industrial, cultural and familial metaprogramming of our own biocomputers.

We all need to awaken beyond the event horizons of our own subjectivity. Otherwise we risk living lives of complete mediocrity and continuing to contribute to the seemingly unending parasitism and destruction of the earth by billions of not-quite-human beings who leap ignorantly, yet all too willingly, into the abyss of ecological and spiritual extinction.

The Center of the Cyclone is not a book which encourages us to approach our awakening and transformation casually. It is not about the irresponsible use of psychedelic substances. It is a primer about researching and probing the vastness of conscious being scientifically, methodically, and even therapeutically. It is a treatise about recognizing that we have all been infected with a

"dis-ease" which is the direct result of systematic societal disassociation from our own all-pervading nature. As such, you will find, it is also about allowing our habitual neuroses and programming to be exposed and transcended and then exposed and transcended again and again as the unfathomable brilliance of our true basic nature opens us to endless wonder.

Needless to say, this book, and all of John's books, have had a major impact on my life. As a twenty-one-year-old man, when I first encountered this volume, a wish arose in my psyche to one day meet and communicate face to face with this wonderfully unconventional scientist and explorer. The Earth Coincidence Control Office (aka ECCO) eventually assured that this should occur.

In June of 1989, John and I both spoke at a large NGO conference held at the United Nations (UN) in New York regarding the future of our planet and the "possible" climatological, sociological, and economic challenges which are the direct result of the unconscious and greedy actions of .00001% of so-called "humans." We now face these catastrophic impacts in the daily news cycle.

As the co-founder (with R. Buckminster Fuller) and director of Project Earth, I was invited to present a rather radical proposal for beginning to heal our relationship to our beleaguered planet and each other. I was also asked to physically demonstrate a remarkable energy-generating technology based on principles demonstrated by

Nikola Tesla in the early 1900s.

John Lilly spoke before me. Every seat in Dag Hammerskjöld Auditorium was completely filled as Dr. Lilly scaled the stairs to the stage. He was dressed in a NASA type jumpsuit that made him look remarkably like the aged astronaut Dr. David Bowman from *2001: A Space Odyssey*. John suddenly tripped and fell onto the stage. Without a blush, he stood back up, walked to the podium, and said, "Now I guess you'll have to decide whether I fell accidentally or intentionally to get your attention. At any rate I got your attention, didn't I?" The audience was his.

Later that day, it was my turn to speak. A former colleague of mine and I were demonstrating that the amount of electrical power that comes out of a solid state electrical device had the potential to be over fifty times the amount it consumes.

At the end of my speech, after a thunderous ovation, it took me nearly an hour to get to the back of the auditorium. Many tearful faces told me that they believed the world would never be the same, that somehow that moment in time would be a positive, revolutionary turning point for the future of Earth. When I reached the door to the lobby, there was John Lilly, smiling from ear to ear. He reached out his hand and said, "I am coming out of retirement to help you get this off the ground. I have been asking why I am still here and now I know. I know we have met in a place beyond all of this, but it is wonderful to see you here. Please accept my help."

What followed was the beginning of an amazing and loving friendship, "in this apparent frame of consciousness and way beyond," as John said. We explored many realms and conspired to find ways to introduce new forms of energy technology and superior modes of consciousness to the needful populations of Earth.

This is neither the time or the place to recall the choreography of events from that point onward but our paths had been joined by unseen hands and we remained friends until he passed from this world.

Once, John asked me which of his books was my first. I told him that I had first read *The Center of the Cyclone*. He nodded. I went on to say that what the conscious process had taught me was that liberation occurs when the "cyclone" gives way to infinite, effortless equanimity and the "center" vanishes into the luminous space of transparent conscious being. He looked over, smiled, and simply said, "Well that's the whole point, isn't it?"

Adam Trombly
Sedona, AZ
December 2016

RECOMMENDED READING

Britain, Dan, *The Godmakers*. New York: Bee-Line Books.

Brown, G. Spencer, *The Laws of Form*. London: Geo. Allen & Unwin.

Castaneda, Carlos, *A Separate Reality*. New York: Simon & Schuster.
The Teachings of Don Juan; a Yaqui way of knowledge. Berkeley, Calif.: University of California Press. New York: Ballantine paperback.

Isherwood, Christopher, *Ramakrishna and His Disciples*. New York: Simon & Schuster. Hollywood, Calif.: Vedanta.

Lilly, M.D., John C. *The Mind of the Dolphin*. New York: Doubleday. New York: Avon paperback.
Programming and Metaprogramming in the Human Biocomputer. Menlo Park, Calif.: Whole Earth Catalog.

Merrell-Wolff, Franklin, *Pathways Through to Space: A Personal Record of Transformation in Consciousness*. New York: Richard R. Smith.

Mishra, M.D., Rammurti S., *The Textbook of Yoga Psychology*, New York: Julian.

Munroe, Robert A., *Journeys Out of the Body*. New York: Doubleday.

Ouspensky, P. D., *The Fourth Way*. New York: Knopf.
    In Search of the Miraculous. New York: Harcourt Brace.

Pearce, Joseph Chilton, *The Crack in the Cosmic Egg*. New York: Julian.

Stapledon, Olaf, *Last & First Men; The Starmaker*. New York: Dover.

Taimni, I. K., *The Science of Yoga*. Wheaton, Ill.: Theosophical Publishing House, Quest paperback.

Tart, Charles T., *Altered States of Consciousness*. New York: John Wiley & Sons.

Van Neumann, John, *The Computer and the Brain*. New Haven, Conn.: Yale University Press.

Watts, Alan, *Nature, Man and Woman*. New York: Random House, Vintage paperback.
    This Is It & Other Essays on Zen & Spiritual Experiences. New York: Pantheon.
    Whole Earth Catalogs and Supplements. Menlo Park, Calif.: Portola Institute.

Yogananda, Paramahansa, *Autobiography of a Yogi*, Los Angeles, Calif.: Self Realization Fellowship

About the Author

John C. Lilly was born January 6, 1915, in St. Paul, Minnesota. He was a graduate of the California Institute of Technology and received his doctorate in medicine from the University of Pennsylvania in 1942. He was a world-renowned scientist who studied and researched projects involving biophysics, neurophysiology, electronics, and neuroanatomy. Dr. Lilly is probably best known for his pioneering research in human-dolphin relations. He was the country's leading authority on the states of solitude, isolation, and confinement and their psychological effects on the human mind.

JOHN C. LILLY, M.D.

John C. Lilly, M.D.
January 6, 1915 – September 30, 2001

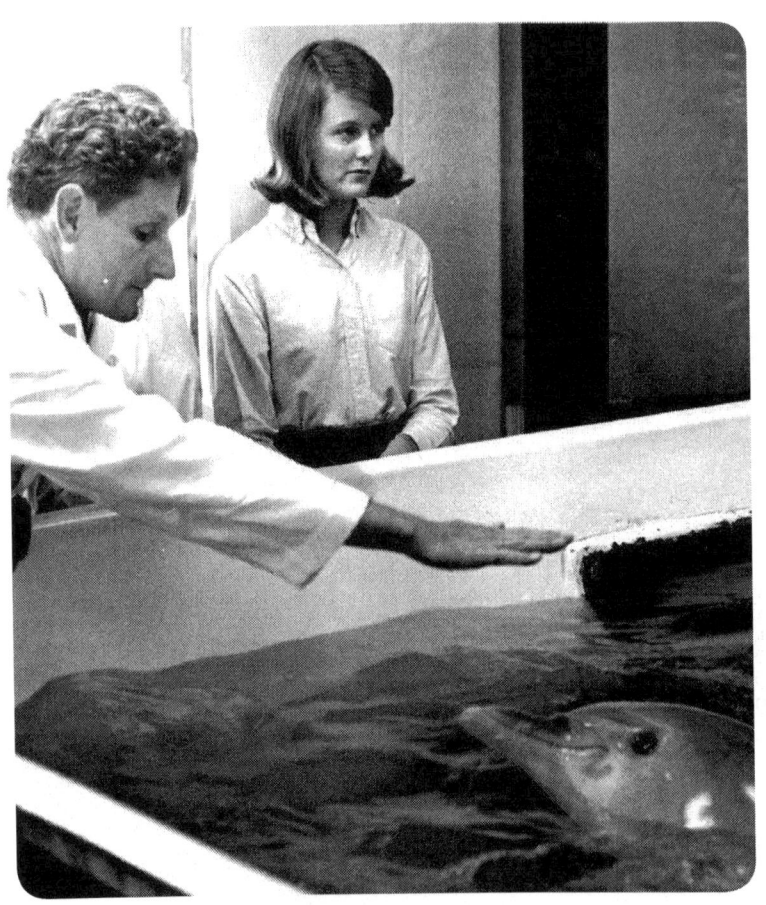

THE CENTER OF THE CYCLONE:
an autobiography of inner space

by John C. Lilly

All rights reserved including the right of reproduction in whole or in part in any form. Copyright the Estate of John C. Lilly 2016.

Special thanks to Philip Hansen Bailey

The typeface used in this book is Aldus, designed by Hermann Zapf in 1954—the same year as the first float tank.

Design & Composition by Graham Talley and Josh Fitz in Portland, OR.

Manufactured in the United States of America.

Coincidence Control Publishing
4530 SE Hawthorne Blvd
Portland, OR 97215

Made in the USA
San Bernardino, CA
29 December 2016